Children's
CLASSIC
STORIES

Fairytales, fables & folktales

First published by Bardfield Press in 2004
Copyright © Miles Kelly Publishing Ltd 2004

Bardfield Press is an imprint of
Miles Kelly Publishing Ltd
Bardfield Centre, Great Bardfield, Essex, CM7 4SL

2 4 6 8 10 9 7 5 3 1

Editorial Director: Anne Marshall
Project Manager: Lisa Clayden
Jacket Design: Debbie Meekcoms
Production Manager: Estela Godoy

British Library Cataloguing-in-Publication Data
A catalogue record for this book is available from the British Library

ISBN 1–84236–384–0

Printed in China

ACKNOWLEDGEMENTS

The publishers would like to thank the following artists
who have contributed to this book:

Julie Banyard, Rosalind Beardshaw, Vanessa Card, Denise Coble, Sally Holmes,
Cecilia Johansson, Stephen Lambert, Priscilla Lamont, Vanessa Lubach,
Gilly Marklew, Diana Mayo, Debbie Meekcoms, A Montgomery–Higham,
Richard Morgan, Tracy Morgan, Tricia Newell, Elizabeth Sawyer,
Susan Scott, Caroline Sharpe, Pam Smy, Pamela Storey–Johnson,
Gwen Tourret, Peter Utton, Mike Walsh, Mike White

www.mileskelly.net
info@mileskelly.net

Children's
CLASSIC
STORIES

Fairytales, fables & folktales

**BARDFIELD
PRESS**

Contents

Animals Big and Small

Boys and Girls

Fairytale Magic

The Magic Porridge Pot

a Swedish folk tale

This is the story of an old porridge pot. One day, just before Christmas, a poor old farmer and his wife decided that they needed to sell their last cow as they had no money left, and no food in the cupboard. As the farmer walked sadly to market with the cow, he met a very strange little man on the road. He had a long white beard right down to his toes, which were bare, and he wore a huge black hat, under which the farmer could only just see the bright gleam of his eyes. Over his arm he carried a battered old porridge pot.

"That's a nice looking cow," said the little man. "Is she for sale?"

"Yes," said the farmer.

"I shall buy your cow," declared the little man, putting the porridge pot down with a thump. "I shall give you this porridge pot in exchange for your cow!"

Well, the farmer looked at the battered old porridge pot, and he looked at his fine cow. And he was just about to say, "Certainly not!" when a voice whispered, "Take me! Take me!"

The farmer shook himself. Dear me, it was bad enough to be poor without beginning to hear strange voices. He opened his mouth again to say, "Certainly not!" when he heard the voice again. "Take me! Take me!"

Well, he saw at once that it must be a magic pot, and he knew you didn't hang about with magic pots, so he said very quickly to the little man, "Certainly!" and handed over the cow. He bent down to pick up the pot, and when he looked up, the little man had vanished into thin air.

The farmer knew he was going to have a difficult time explaining to his wife just how he had come to part with their precious cow for a battered old porridge pot.

She was very angry indeed and had started to say a lot of very cross things when a voice came from the pot,

"Take me inside and clean me and polish me, and you shall see what you shall see!"

Well, the farmer's wife was astonished but she did as she was bid. She washed the pot inside and out, and then she polished it until it shone as bright as a new pin. No sooner had she finished than the pot hopped off the table, and straight out of the door. The farmer and his wife sat down by the fire, not saying a word to each other.

They had no money, no cow, no food and now it seemed they didn't even have their magic pot.

Down the road from the poor farmer, there lived a rich man. He was a selfish man who spent all his time eating huge meals and counting his money. He had lots of servants, including a cook who was in the kitchen making a Christmas pudding. The pudding was stuffed with plums, currants, sultanas, almonds and goodness knows what else. It was so big that the cook realised she didn't have a pot to boil it in. It was at this point that the porridge pot trotted in the door.

"Goodness me!" she exclaimed. "The fairies must have sent this pot just in time to take my pudding," and she dropped the pudding in the pot. No sooner had the pudding fallen to the bottom with a very satisfying thud, than the pot skipped out of the door again. The cook gave a great shriek, but by the time the butler and the footman and the parlour maid and the boy who turned the spit had all dashed into the kitchen, the pot was quite out of sight.

The porridge pot in the meantime trotted down the road to the poor farmer's house. He and his wife were delighted to see the pot again, and even more pleased when they discovered the wonderful pudding. The wife boiled it up and it lasted them for three days. So they had a good Christmas after all, while the old porridge pot sat quietly by the fire.

Spring came, and still the porridge pot sat quietly by the fire. Then one day the pot suddenly trotted over to the farmer's wife and said,

"Clean me, and polish me, and you shall see what you shall see."

So the farmer's wife polished the pot till it shone as bright as a new pin.

No sooner had she finished than the pot hopped off the table, and straight out of the door.

You will remember that the rich man was very fond of counting his money. There he sat in the great hall, with piles of golden guineas and silver sixpences on the table, and great bulging bags of coins on the floor at his feet. He was wondering where he could hide the money when in trotted the pot. Now the cook had been far too frightened of the rich man's temper to tell him about the pot stealing the Christmas pudding, so when he saw the pot he was delighted.

"Goodness me!" he exclaimed, "The fairies must have sent this pot just in time to take my money," and he dropped several bags of money in the pot. No sooner had the bags fallen to the bottom with a very satisfying clink, than the pot skipped out of the door again. The rich man shouted and hollered, but by the time the coachman and the head groom and the stable lad had run into the great hall, the pot was quite out of sight.

It trotted down the road to the poor farmer's house. He and his wife were delighted to see the pot again, and even more pleased when they discovered the bags of gold and silver. There was enough money to last them for the rest of their days, even after they had bought a new cow.

As for the battered old porridge pot, it sat quietly by the fire for many a long year. Then, one day, it suddenly trotted straight out of the door. It went off up the road until it was out of sight, and the farmer and his wife never saw it again.

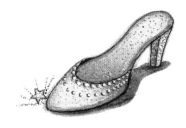

Cinderella

a retelling from the original tale by Charles Perrault

O nce upon a time, when there were still fairy godmothers, there was a girl called Cinderella. She lived with her father and his new wife, and her two new step-sisters. The step-mother did not like Cinderella very much, mostly because she was so much nicer than her own two daughters. Cinderella was also much prettier. Oh, but the step-sisters were ugly!

Cinderella had to do all the work in the house as the ugly sisters were also very lazy. They spent all the father's money on new clothes and endless pairs of shoes, and then

went off to parties leaving poor
Cinderella with piles of stockings
to mend.

One day a very grand
invitation arrived. The prince was
looking for a wife, and had
decided to give a ball in three
days time for all the young ladies
in the land. The ugly sisters could
talk about nothing else. They
bought lots of new dresses and many pairs of matching
shoes, and then spent every hour trying them all on. They
made Cinderella curl their hair and iron their ribbons and
powder their noses. Cinderella was so exhausted running
around after them that she had no time to look into her
own wardrobe to choose what she should wear.

In a waft of perfume, the ugly sisters swept out of the

door into the carriage without as much as a thank you to Cinderella. She closed the door sadly, and went to sit by the fire in the kitchen.

"I wish I could have gone to the ball, too," she sighed.

There was a sudden swirl of silver stars, and there in front of Cinderella stood an old lady with a twinkle in her eye, and a wand in her hand.

"You shall go to the ball, my dear Cinderella. I am your fairy godmother," she said, smiling at Cinderella. "Now, we must be quick, there is much to do! Please bring me a large pumpkin from the vegetable patch. Oh, and six mice from the barn, and you will find four lizards by the water butt."

Cinderella did as she was bid. With a wave of the wand, the pumpkin was turned into a glittering golden coach and the mice into six pure white horses. The lizards became elegant footmen, dressed in green velvet.

"Now you, my dear," said the fairy godmother, turning to Cinderella. A wave of the wand, and Cinderella's old apron disappeared and there she stood in a white dress, glittering with golden stars. Her hair was piled on top of her head and it too was sprinkled with stars. On her feet were tiny glass slippers with diamonds in the heels.

"Enjoy yourself, my dear," said the fairy godmother, "but you must leave before midnight for then my magic ends and you will be back in your old apron with some mice and lizards at your feet!"

When Cinderella arrived at the ball everyone turned to look at this unknown beauty who had arrived so unexpectedly. The prince hurried over to ask her to dance and then would not dance with anyone else all evening. The ugly sisters were beside themselves with rage, which of course made them look even uglier.

Cinderella was enjoying herself so much that she forgot the fairy godmother's warning, so she had a terrible fright when the clock began to strike midnight. She turned from the prince with a cry and ran down the stairs of the palace into her carriage, and disappeared as suddenly as she had arrived. One of the tiny glass slippers with diamonds sparkling in the heels had slipped from her foot as she ran. The prince picked it up and turning to the crowded ballroom declared, "I shall marry the girl whose foot fits this slipper!"

Cinderella, meanwhile, had just managed to reach her

garden gate when all her finery disappeared, and by the time the ugly sisters arrived home, both in a towering rage, she was sitting quietly by the fire.

The next morning, the prince went from house to house looking for the mystery girl whose foot would fit the tiny glass slipper. But no one had feet that small. He reached Cinderella's house where first one ugly sister and then the next tried to squash their huge feet into the slipper.

"Please let me try," said a quiet voice from the corner, and Cinderella stepped forward.

The sisters just laughed in scorn but they soon stopped when they saw that the tiny slipper fitted Cinderella perfectly. There was a sudden swirl of silver stars, and there in front of Cinderella stood her fairy godmother with a twinkle in her eye, and a wand in her hand. In an instant, Cinderella was clothed in a gorgeous dress of cornflower blue silk decorated with pearls. On her feet she wore tiny white boots with blue tassels.

The prince whisked Cinderella off to the palace to meet the king and queen, and the wedding took place the very next day. Cinderella forgave the two ugly sisters, she was that sort of girl. But the prince insisted the sisters spent one day a week working in the palace kitchens just to remind them how horrid they had been to Cinderella.

Snow White and Rose Red

a retelling from the original story by the Brothers Grimm

Once upon a time there was a widow who had two daughters, Snow White and Rose Red. Snow White was quiet and gentle, Rose Red was wild as the hills, but they loved each other, and their mother, so the little house in the woods was a happy one.

One winter's evening as they all sat round the fire there was a knock at the door. Rose Red opened it and gave a scream. There stood a great big brown bear! But in a deep rumbly voice the bear said,

"Please do not be afraid. All I ask is that you let me sleep by your fire tonight. It is so cold outside."

"Of course you may shelter with us," said the mother. And she called the girls to set the soup on the stove and to put another log on the fire.

"Would you brush the snow from my fur, please?" asked the bear. Rose Red fetched the big broom and carefully brushed the bear's great shaggy coat. Snow White gave him a great bowl of hot soup and the bear gulped it down in one. Then he stretched out in front of the fire and was soon fast asleep.

In the morning Snow White let him out of the cottage and he padded off into the forest through the deep snow. But in the evening, he returned and once again Snow White and Rose Red and their mother looked after him. After that the bear came every night all through the winter, and they all grew very fond of him. But when spring came, the bear told them he would not be returning any more.

"I have to guard my treasure. Once the snows have melted all kinds of wicked people try to steal it," he said and giving them all a hug he set off through the forest. Just as he passed through the garden gate, his fur caught on a nail. For a fleeting moment Snow White thought she saw a glint of gold, but the bear hurried off and was soon out of sight.

A few days later, Rose Red and Snow White were out gathering berries to make jam when they came alongside a fallen tree. Then they saw a very cross dwarf, tugging at his beard which was trapped by the great tree trunk.

"Well, don't stand there like a pair of silly geese! Come and help me!" he shrieked.

Well, no matter how hard they tugged Rose Red and

Snow White were not strong enough to lift the tree, so
Rose Red took her scissors out and snipped off the end

of the dwarf's beard.

He was absolutely
furious, and snatched up
a big bag of gold from
the tree roots and
disappeared without a
word of thanks.

Some days later the girls' mother said she really
fancied a piece of fish for supper, so they went down to the
river to see what they could catch. But instead of a fish,
they found their friend the cross dwarf again. This time his
beard was all caught up in his fishing line.

"Don't just stand there gawping," he yelled, "help me
get free!"

Snow White tried to untangle it but it was impossible

so she too snipped a piece off his beard. He was quite white with rage, but just grasped a casket of jewels that lay at the water's edge and turned away without a word of thanks.

It was the Spring Fair a few days later. The girls decided to go and buy some new ribbons for their hats, and their mother wanted needles for her embroidery, so they set off early in the morning. They had not gone far when they heard a terrible shrieking and crying. They ran towards the sound, and there once more was the cross dwarf, this time struggling in the huge talons of an eagle. They tugged and tugged and the eagle had to let go.

"You have torn my coat," muttered the ungrateful dwarf and picked up a basket of pearls and hobbled off as fast as possible. The girls just laughed and continued on their way to the fair.

They had a wonderful time, and it was quite late

when they walked slowly home. The sun was just sinking behind a big rock when, to their astonishment, they came across the dwarf again. There spread out on the ground in front of him was a great pile of gold and precious jewels and pearls.

Suddenly the dwarf saw Snow White and Rose Red.

"Go away! Go away! You horrid girls are always in my way," he shouted. But just then there was a huge growl and the great brown bear stood by their side. With one huge paw he swiped the dwarf up, up into the sky and no one ever saw where he fell to earth again. The bear turned towards Snow White and Rose Red and as they looked,

his great shaggy coat fell away. There stood a handsome young man, dressed in a golden suit of the richest velvet.

"Do not be afraid, Snow White and Rose Red," he said smiling. "Now you can see who I really am. That wicked dwarf put a spell on me so he could steal all my treasure, but you have broken the spell by your kindness."

They all went home, laden with the treasure. They talked long into the night, and it was all still true the next morning! Snow White married the handsome young man who, by great good fortune, had a younger brother who married Rose Red, so they all lived happily ever after.

But if you ever find a dwarf with half his beard missing, I would be very careful if I were you.

Rumpelstiltskin

a retelling from the original tale by the Brothers Grimm

O nce upon a time there was a miller. He was a foolish man who was always boasting. Then he went too far.

The king was riding past the mill with his huntsmen one day. The miller's daughter was sitting in the doorway, spinning. The king noticed that she was a pretty girl so he began talking to her. Her father came bustling up and began to tell the king what a splendid daughter she was.

"Why, your Majesty, she can even spin straw into gold!" boasted the ridiculous miller.

Needless to say, the poor girl could do nothing of the
sort but the king thought this was an excellent way to refill
the palace treasure house which was rather empty, so he
took her back to the palace. He put her in a room with a
great pile of straw and told her he wanted to see it all spun
into gold the next morning, or else it would be the worse
for her.

As soon as the door was
locked she began to cry.
The task was impossible.
Then she heard a
thin little voice.

"Do stop crying!
You will make the straw all wet, and then we will have no
chance of turning it into gold!"

There in front of her stood a strange little man. He
had a tiny round body with long skinny legs and huge

feet. His clothes looked as if they had seen better days, and on his head he wore a tall battered-looking hat.

"If you give me your necklace, I will do what the king has asked of you," he snapped.

The miller's daughter unclasped her necklace and handed it to the little man. He hid it deep in one of his pockets, and sat down by the spinning wheel. The spinning wheel turned in a blur. The pile of straw grew smaller, and the mound of shining gold grew higher. As the first light of day shone in through the window it was all done. The strange little man disappeared as suddenly as he had appeared. The king was delighted with the great pile of gold, and asked the miller's daughter to marry him. She was too shy to reply so the king just took her silence as her agreement and married her anyway that afternoon.

For a while all was well. But then the treasure house grew empty again so once more the poor girl, now the queen, was locked in a room with a pile of straw and a spinning wheel.

As the queen wept, once more the strange little man appeared. The queen asked him to help her again, and offered him all the rich jewels she was wearing. But the strange little man was not interested in jewels this time.

"You must promise to give me your first born child," he whispered.

The queen was desperate. But she promised and the little man sat down at the spinning wheel. A great pile of gold appeared by the side of the spinning wheel, and by dawn the straw had all gone. The king was delighted and for a while all was well. Then the queen gave birth to a beautiful baby, and she remembered with dread her promise to the strange little man. Seven days after the baby was born, he appeared by the side of the cradle. The queen wept and wept.

"There you go again," said the little man crossly. "always crying!"

"I will do anything but let you have my baby," cried the queen.

"Very well then, anything to make you stop crying." said the little man, who by now was dripping wet from all the queen's tears. "If you can guess my name in three days, I will let you keep your baby," he said and disappeared as suddenly as he had appeared.

The next morning the little man appeared by the side of the cradle. The queen had sent messengers out far and wide to see if anyone knew the strange little man's name.

"Is it Lacelegs?" she asked.

"No!"

"Is it Wimbleshanks?"

"No!"

"Is it Bandyknees?"

"No!"

and the little man disappeared as suddenly as he had appeared. The queen sent out even more messengers to the lands far beyond the borders of the kingdom. The second morning the strange little man appeared by the side of the cradle.

"Is it Bluenose?" the queen asked.

"No!"

"Is it Longtooth?"

"No!"

"Is it Skinnyribs?"

"No!" and the little man disappeared with a nasty laugh.

The queen waited up all night as her messengers came in one by one, and just as she was giving up all hope of saving her precious baby, in came the very last one. He was utterly exhausted but he brought the queen the best of news. In a deep, deep, dark forest he had found a strange little man dancing round a fire, singing this song.

Today I brew, today I bake,

Tomorrow I will the baby take.

The queen will lose the game,

Rumpelstiltskin is my name!

The strange little man appeared by the cradle. The queen pretended she still did not know his name.

"Is it Gingerteeth?" she asked.

"No!" said the little man, and he picked the baby up.

"Is is Silverhair?" asked the queen.

"No!" said the little man, and he started to walk towards the door, with a wicked smile.

"Is it Rumpelstiltskin?" asked the queen, and she ran up to the strange little man.

"Some witch told you that!" shrieked the little man, and he stamped his foot so hard that he fell through the floor and was never seen again. The queen told the king the whole story and he was so pleased his baby and his queen were safe that he forgot to be cross with the miller who had told such a terrible fib in the first place!

The Elves and the Shoemaker

a retelling from the original story by the Brothers Grimm

There was a time when everyone believed in elves. The shoemaker and his wife in this story certainly did!

The shoemaker worked hard from morn to night. The shoes he made were of the finest leather, and he was good with his hands, but business was slow. One night he found he only had enough leather left for one more pair of shoes. With a heavy heart, he cut the leather and left the pieces ready to sew the next morning. He blew out the candle, and crossed the yard from his little shop into the house.

"Wife, I do not know what we shall do. I have just cut out the very last piece of leather in the shop," he said sadly.

"Don't be too gloomy, husband," said his wife with a tired smile. "Perhaps you will be able to sell this last pair of shoes for a fine price. Wait and see what tomorrow brings!"

The next day the shoemaker was up early as usual. When he pulled back the shutters in the shop, you can imagine his surprise when he  saw not pieces of leather ready to sew on the bench, but a fine pair of ladies' shoes with delicate pointed toes. The stitching was so fine you would think it had been done by mice. He put the shoes in the window of the shop, and before long a rich merchant came in and bought the shoes for his new wife, paying the poor shoemaker double the usual price. The shoemaker was delighted at this turn in his fortunes, and bought enough leather to make two new pairs of shoes.

Once again, he cut the leather carefully, and left the pieces ready on his work bench to sew the next morning

The next day the shoemaker was up even earlier than usual. His wife came with him as he went into the shop, and pulled back the shutters.

"Oh husband," she gasped, for there on the bench stood two pairs of the finest shoes she had ever seen. There was a green pair with red heels, and a pair so shiny and black the shoemaker could see his face in them. He put the shoes in the window, and very quickly in came a poet who bought the green pair with red heels, and not far behind him there was a parson who bought the shiny black pair.

And both paid him a great deal of money for the splendid shoes with stitching so fine you would think it had been done by mice.

This continued for many days. The shoemaker would buy new leather and leave the pieces cut ready on his bench at night, and when he came back in the morning there would be the most exquisite shoes. The shoemaker's reputation spread, and his shop was soon full of customers, anxious to buy his special shoes. Before long the shoemaker and his wife were no longer poor, but they still lived simply as they had little wish for the luxuries of life. It was enough to be happy and healthy. One day, the wife said, "Husband, I think we must see who it is who has given us this great good fortune so we may thank them."

The shoemaker agreed, so that night after laying out

the cut leather pieces and blowing out the candle, he and his wife hid behind the door of the shop. As the town hall clock struck midnight, they heard a scampering of tiny feet and little voices, laughing. Two tiny elves slid out from behind the skirting board and climbed up onto the bench where they were soon hard at work, stitching away with tiny stitches that were so fine they might have been done by mice. The elves sang as they stitched, sitting cross-legged on the bench. But 'oh!' they looked poor. Their trousers were ragged, their shirts were threadbare and their poor feet looked frozen as they had neither socks nor shoes. In a twinkling of an eye all the leather was used up, and there on the bench stood many pairs of shoes. The elves slipped away, laughing as they went.

The shoemaker and his wife looked at each other, and then and there both decided to reward the little craftsmen. The next day, the shoemaker took some scraps of green and yellow leather and, with the tiniest stitches possible, he made two little pairs of boots, yellow with green heels. The wife took her sewing basket and some scraps of cloth and, with the tiniest stitches possible, made two little pairs of red velvet trousers and two smart green jackets with shiny silver buttons. Then she knitted two little pairs of yellow socks, with the tiniest stitches possible.

That night, the shoemaker did not cut out any leather. Instead he laid out the clothes and the boots with the socks, and once again he and his wife hid behind the door of the shop.

As the town hall clock struck midnight, they heard a scampering of tiny feet and little voices, laughing. The two tiny elves slid out from behind the skirting board and climbed up onto the bench. When they saw the gifts, they clapped their hands in delight and, laughing merrily, flung off their old rags and tried on their new clothes and the boots. They looked splendid. Still laughing and smiling, they slipped away behind the skirting board, and the shoemaker and his wife never saw them ever again.

But once a year when the shoemaker opened the shop in the morning, on his bench he would find a special pair of shoes with stitching so fine you would think it had been done by mice.

The Three Wishes

an English folk tale

There was once a poor fisherman who lived by the edge of the sea in a tumbledown old cottage. He lived with his wife, who was always grumbling no matter how hard and long the fisherman worked.

One evening he threw the nets out for one last try before it grew dark. He had caught nothing all day. As he began pulling the nets in the fisherman's hopes rose: the nets were heavy. But when he hauled them in there was only one tiny fish lying at the bottom. Then the fish spoke. The fisherman rubbed his eyes in astonishment.

"Please throw me back into the sea," said the fish. "I am so small I would not make much of a meal for you."

But the fisherman was tired and hungry.

"Even though you are small I cannot throw you back. My wife would not be pleased if I came home empty handed." he said with a deep sigh.

"I will grant you the first three wishes made in your cottage if you let me go," said the fish, "but I should warn you that wishes do not always give you what you really want."

Well, the fisherman did not hear the fish's warning. All he heard was the bit about three wishes, and he thought that finally his grumbling wife could have whatever she wanted. So he carefully untangled the tiny fish from the nets and placed it back in the sea. With a flick of its tail the fish disappeared deep, deep under water.

The fisherman ran all the way home and in great excitement told her all about the tiny fish. But instead of being pleased, she just shouted at him as usual.

"Trust you to believe such a thing! Whoever heard of a talking fish, you must be daft husband," and she slammed down a plate of dry bread and a rind of cheese in front of the poor fisherman.

"I wish this was a plate of fine sausages, I am so hungry," said the fisherman wistfully.

No sooner were the words out of his mouth than there was a wonderful smell and there in front of him was a plate of sizzling sausages! He was delighted and reached for his knife when his wife yelled at him,

"Why couldn't you have wished for something better? We could have had chests of gold and fine clothes to wear!" and this from the woman who had refused to believe his story only a few moments before. "You stupid fool! I wish the sausages were at the end of your nose!"

There was a ghastly silence as the wife looked at her poor husband. Hanging from the end of his nose was a great string of sausages. The fisherman remembered what the fish had said – the first three wishes made in the cottage.

The fisherman and his wife pulled and pulled at the sausages, but it was no good. They were stuck fast. There was nothing for it, they would have to use the last wish.

"I wish the sausages would disappear," said the fisherman sadly, and they did in a flash. So there they sat, the poor fisherman and his grumbling wife. No delicious supper of sizzling sausages and, much worse, no magic wishes. The fisherman never caught the tiny fish again, and as far as I know, his wife never stopped grumbling. Wishes do not always give you what you really want.

The Pot of Gold

an Irish folk tale

Niall O'Leary was sitting on a gate in the sunshine, day-dreaming quite happily, when – TIC! TIC! TIC! – he became aware of a sharp sound coming from the field behind him.

"Now what on earth can that be?" Niall wondered to himself. "It's too loud to be a grasshopper . . . and it's too quiet to be a bird."

TIC! TIC! TIC! it went.

Niall O'Leary swung his legs over the gate and turned around. He blinked in astonishment. There in the long grass of the field was the tiniest man Niall had ever seen, no higher than his boot. The tiny man had his back to Niall, but Niall could see that he was dressed all in green, with a long white feather in his cap. A tiny leather shoe lay before him on a rock, and he was banging away at it with a tiny stone hammer.

Niall's eyes lit up. A leprechaun! A real, live leprechaun! Niall licked his lips greedily. Every tiny leprechaun had a huge pot of gold hidden somewhere. And as everybody knew, if you caught hold of a leprechaun and squeezed him tightly enough, he would have to tell you where his treasure was buried.

Quietly, quietly, Niall O'Leary got down from the gate.

TIC! TIC! TIC! went the leprechaun's hammer.

Quietly, quietly, Niall O'Leary crept through the grass.

TIC! TIC! TIC! went the leprechaun's hammer.

Quietly, quietly, Niall O'Leary reached out with his large, meaty hands . . .

"GOTCHA!" cried Niall O'Leary, and he squeezed and squeezed the wriggling leprechaun with all his might.

"Oooooof!" cried the leprechaun. "Let me go, you big bully!"

"Tell me where your gold is and I will!" boomed Niall.

"I can't tell you anything while you're squeezing the breath out of me," the leprechaun gasped, looking rather purple.

"Oops, sorry!" blustered Niall, and relaxed his grip.

"That's better," wheezed the leprechaun, taking gulps of air. "Now put me down and I promise I'll show you where my gold is hidden."

A broad grin spread across Niall's face as he lowered the leprechaun back down to the grass. "A leprechaun can't break his promise!" he chuckled.

"No," grumbled the leprechaun rather crossly, "and my gold is buried under here." He leapt a few steps into the middle of the field and pointed at a clump of dandelions. "You'll need a spade, mind," the leprechaun added thoughtfully. "You'll have to dig quite a way down."

Niall's face fell. "But I haven't got a spade with me," he said, glumly. "What shall I do?"

"Why don't you tie your handkerchief around the dandelions so you don't forget where the gold is buried," the leprechaun suggested.

"Then hurry back home and fetch a spade. I promise on my word of honour that I won't untie the handkerchief."

Niall's face brightened once again. "What a great idea!" he beamed. He fumbled in his pocket, brought out a rather grubby red silk handkerchief, and tied it around the clump of dandelions. It waved at him in the breeze like a cheerful flag. "Thank you Mr Leprechaun," Niall remembered to say politely. "You've been mighty helpful." Then in a few strides, he was back over the gate and away home, humming merrily.

As soon as Niall had grabbed the biggest spade he could find in the garden shed, he set off back to the field at once. All the way down the lane, he day-dreamed of what he would do with the gold. But when Niall O'Leary reached the gate, he stopped stone-still and his mouth hung open. He dropped the spade and scratched his head. "Well, blow me down," gasped Niall. All over the field, thousands of red silk handkerchiefs were tied onto clumps of dandelions and fluttering in the breeze. And Niall could hear the sound of gleeful leprechaun laughter floating over the grass on the wind.

So Niall O'Leary never got his pot of gold after all. But that is how he came to own the most successful silk handkerchief shop in the whole of Ireland . . .

The Wild Swans

a retelling from the original story by Hans Christian Andersen

A long time ago, in a land far away, there lived a king whose wife died, leaving him with eleven little sons and a baby daughter, Elise. The king married again and the children's new stepmother was cruel and jealous. She seemed to put the king under a wicked spell which made him forget all about his beloved children. So the queen sent little Elise away from the palace to be brought up by a peasant couple who lived in the forest. Then she used witchcraft to turn the princes into swans and she sent them flying off from the palace forever.

Many years passed and Elise thought she would never see her brothers again. Then one evening, as she was sitting by a lake watching the sun set, she saw a line of swans come flying like a white ribbon across the sky. They alighted next to her, and at the exact moment when the sun melted into the lake, the swans disappeared in a flutter of feathers. In their place stood eleven princes. They were Elise's long-lost brothers! They recognised each other at once, and they ran to hug each other, weeping tears of joy.

"We have to live as swans by day," the princes explained, "but at night we return to our true selves. Our wicked stepmother banished us to live in a country which lies across a wide sea and we are only allowed to return here once a year for just eleven days. Tomorrow is the day that we must leave once again. Little sister, it is a dangerous journey, but now we have found you, we will take you with us."

All night long, the princes gathered willow bark and tough reeds and rushes and Elise wove them into a strong net. By sunrise, as the princes fluttered back into swans, Elise was lying in the woven mesh, fast asleep. The swans seized the net strings and, with a few powerful wingbeats, sped off into the sky. And so the brothers carried their sister, right across the land and over the churning sea . . .

High above the waves, Elise dreamed she saw a beautiful fairy who smiled sadly and said, "If you are very brave, you can set your brothers free from their enchantment. You must go to the churchyard and pick the stinging nettles that grow on the graves there. They will burn and blister your skin, but you must pick them with your bare hands and then crush them with your bare feet. Twine the nettles into flax and weave eleven shirts with long sleeves. The second that you throw the shirts over your brothers, they will be swans no longer. But mark this well, from the moment you start your task, you must not speak. If you utter a single word, it will be like a dagger through your brothers' hearts and they will surely die."

Elise awoke with a start to find herself lying on a bed of moss in a great cavern, shaded with vines and creepers. Her brothers were flown, and strangely there was a stinging nettle lying next to her. At once, she slipped away to find the churchyard. The graves were silent and spooky, but Elise clambered all over them collecting the nettles that sprang there in thick clumps. How the nettles burnt and blistered her hands! Elise hurried back to the cave and trampled on the nettles until they were crushed and her feet swollen and sore. Finally, she twisted the stalks into flax and began carefully to weave . . .

Elise's work was clumsy and slow due to her red, painful hands and arms. But by the evening when the swans returned, she had woven nearly half of the first shirt. The princes were upset by Elise's strange task and scared by her silence. But when they saw the spark of hope in Elise's eyes, they realised that she must be suffering for their sake. The youngest brother wept for his sister's pain, and as his tears fell onto her injured arms and hands, the blisters healed themselves and disappeared.

Elise would have worked around the clock, until all eleven shirts were finished and the spell finally broken. However, the next day, her hiding place in the cavern was sniffed out by hunting dogs and a royal hunting party burst in upon her. Elise was terrified, but she knew that if she uttered a single word, her brothers would die. The king thought that Elise was the most beautiful girl he had ever seen. "Don't be afraid," he said gently to her, as she stood

trembling and silent. "Whoever you are, you can't live here
in this cave. You will come back to my palace and I will
make sure you are looked after and taken care of." The

king lifted Elise up behind
him on his horse and
they were off like the
wind over the hills.
Elise wept

without a word as the ladies
of the court dressed her in silks and satins, threaded pearls
in her hair, and led her into a splendid banquet which the
king had ordered in her honour. "You will be my queen,"
the king told Elise gently after the feast, "but I do not want
you to be sad. I want you to be happy here with me." The
king led Elise down a corridor to a small door. He opened
it and Elise's mouth widened into a perfect "O" of surprise.
The room was adorned with green hangings, to look just

like the cave in the forest. And on the floor was the shirt she had finished and all the bundles of nettles from the churchyard. Elise flung her arms around the king and kissed his face and hands as he handed her the key to the little room.

After that, Elise spent every day at the king's side. She could see that he was good and kind and thoughtful, and she longed to tell him how much she had begun to care for him – but she dared not utter a sound. Every night, Elise crept down the corridor in her nightdress to her secret little room and continued with her weaving. Her heart was heavy with the thought that her brothers did not know where she was and must be searching anxiously for her.

Night after night, the pile of flax grew lower and lower, and by the time the tenth shirt was finished, Elise was in desperate need of more nettles. There was nothing for it but to creep out of the palace by moonlight, and hurry down the dark paths all the way to the churchyard. When Elise reached the graves, her blood ran cold with horror. Witches sat on the tombstones, reaching down into the earth with their bony fingers. Elise thought of her brothers and forced herself to walk past the witches and collect huge armfuls of the burning nettles. Then she was away, hurrying back to the palace before dawn . . .

Unbeknown to Elise, the king's chief advisor had spied on her. He had always been jealous of the wild, silent girl from the cave who had won the king's heart and now sat at the king's side instead of him. His wicked heart leapt for joy as he hurried to the king the very next morning.

"Your majesty," the chief advisor whispered,

"I am sorry to tell you that I saw your bride-to-be at the churchyard last night, surrounded by witches. She can only have been performing black magic."

The king shook his head vigorously. "You must be mistaken," he said. "I do not believe it."

"Go to Elise's room and see the new pile of churchyard nettles she collected for her spells," the chief advisor insisted. "She is a witch and she must be burnt. The people will find out and they will demand it."

The king hung his head in sorrow. He felt as though his heart was breaking.

Next morning, guards broke into Elise's chamber and hauled her away to a dark, damp prison. They left her with only her nettles for a pillow and the shirts she had woven to keep her warm but they were all Elise wanted. Elise didn't know what she had done wrong, but she knew she was going to die and that she didn't have much time left. Her hands trembled as she hurried desperately to finish the final shirt. As she twisted and plaited and wove, a swan came flapping his wings against the window. Elise recognised her youngest brother and she ran to thrust her fingers through the bars and stroke his feathers. She couldn't say a word to tell him what had happened, and tears sparkled in her eyes as she waved him away and hurried back to her work . . .

All day and all night, Elise's sore fingers worked faster than ever. As the sun's rays stretched through the bars, the final shirt was nearly, nearly finished . . . Elise didn't stop frantically working even when the guards thrust her into a smelly cart and they went bumping through the streets. Crowds of people threw mud at her and jeered.

"Look at the witch!" they shouted. "See, she's working on some evil spell!"

Then the cart arrived at the bonfire and the executioner stepped forwards to drag Elise to her death. But suddenly, eleven huge white swans swooped down out of the sky. Quick as a flash, Elise grabbed the shirts and threw them over the birds.

The crowd fell back in terror as there was a huge flash of lightning. The swans disappeared and in their places stood eleven handsome princes – although the youngest had a swan's wing instead of one arm, for Elise had run out of time to finish the final sleeve of his shirt.

"Now I can speak!" Elise sobbed. "I am innocent!" She sank into her brothers' arms and the princes explained all that had happened. Then the people began to cheer and the church bells rang out for joy, and the king took his beautiful bride and her brothers back home to his palace.

The Pied Piper of Hamelin

an Irish folk tale

I magine what it would be like to live in a town overrun by rats. Rats in the streets, the shops, the gardens! Rats in the town hall, the hospital and police station! Rats in your school corridors, your classroom, your desk! Rats in your kitchen, your bath, your bed! Well, that's what it was like to live in the town of Hamelin, which lay beside the River Weser.

No one knew where the rats had come from or how they had managed to take over the town in such numbers. The townspeople of Hamelin were desperate to be rid of them. They couldn't eat without rats nibbling off their plates. They couldn't get dressed without uncovering rats nesting in their clothes and boots. They couldn't put their babies down to sleep without finding rats cuddled up in the cradles. They couldn't even chat to each other in comfort, for the noise of all the squeaking and scampering! So you can see why the mayor put up a poster outside the town hall saying:

There will be a reward of

ONE THOUSAND GUILDERS

to anyone who can get rid of the rats!

Yes, one thousand guilders! Everyone began to imagine what they would do with such a huge fortune – but of course, they could only dream. No one had the first idea how to begin claiming their town back from the rats.

By the time the stranger came knocking on the door of the town hall, the mayor was panic-stricken. He would have listened to anybody who said they could help. So when the stranger announced confidently, "I can get rid of all the rats for you," the mayor didn't worry too much about the stranger's odd, multicoloured costume. The mayor paid no attention to the stranger's extraordinarily long fingers and the unusual pipe that hung on a cord round his neck. The mayor didn't think too much about the sad smile on the stranger's face or the wistful gleam in his eyes. The mayor just beamed with relief and said, "GREAT! When can you begin?"

"Right now," replied the stranger, and he raised his pipe to his lips. Off he went, out of the town hall and into the street, playing a lilting tune that filled the air. Instantly, the rats stopped scuffling, pricked up their ears, and listened. For the first time in many, many months, there was silence for a moment. Then the scampering and squeaking began again, as the rats followed the Pied Piper.

The townspeople of Weser couldn't believe their eyes.

All through the town strolled the Pied Piper, his fingers
continually moving on his pipe and the haunting notes
rippling through the air. And out of all the houses swarmed
the rats; out of every garden and gutter,
out of every nook and cranny they
came streaming. Down stairwells and
through streets, out of passages and
alleyways, over rooftops and along roads the
rats came hurrying after the strange
musician. And the Pied Piper didn't
stop playing all the way to the
wide River Weser. He
didn't stop
playing as

he dipped one brightly coloured foot into the rushing waters and the thousands of rats began to plunge off the bank into the river. He didn't stop playing until the very last rat had drowned.

Then the church bells rang out in celebration, the townspeople started hugging each other, the children began dancing and singing – and the Pied Piper strode quietly back to the town hall to fetch his reward.

"My one thousand guilders, if you please," said the Pied Piper, calmly.

The mayor just smiled what he thought was a charming smile. Now the rats were dead and gone he certainly didn't plan on giving away what was nearly the entire contents of the town council bank account! "Come, come now, my dear fellow," the mayor coaxed. "One thousand guilders is somewhat over-the-top for playing a pretty ditty on a tin whistle, surely you'll agree! Why don't we settle on fifty guilders, and I'll throw in a nice bronze medal and even put up a statue of you and me together in the market place, eh?"

The Pied Piper simply turned on his heel and walked out into the street. As he went, he once more lifted his pipe to his lips. But this time, he played a different tune. Enchanting notes rippled all around and down the roads the children came dancing, running and leaping after the Pied Piper.

The men and women of Hamelin were struck still with horror as the children swept past them and were gone through the town. Playing his strange melody, the Pied Piper led the children past the River Weser and skipping happily along a path that led up to a steep, craggy mountain. He piped a burst of airy notes and a little door appeared in the mountain slope. The Pied Piper led the children inside. The townspeople could hear the echo of his pipe and the children's laughter grow fainter and fainter as they went deeper and deeper into the earth. Then suddenly, the little door slammed shut and disappeared. The children were gone – all except for one little boy who was lame and so hadn't been able to keep up with the others. He stood on the mountainside and sobbed, calling out for his friends. But the little door had vanished.

No one ever saw the Pied Piper or the children again. But on sunny days, some townsfolk swore they could hear ripples of childish laughter floating down from the mountain. And from that day to this, there has never been a single rat in the town of Hamelin.

Belle and the Beast

a retelling from the original tale by Madame Leprince de Beaumont

There was once a businessman who had made a fortune by trading overseas. He lived in a magnificent mansion staffed by servants and with a TV in every room – including the indoor swimming pool. The businessman's wife had died, so he had brought up their three beautiful daughters on his own.

Unfortunately, the two eldest girls, Bianca and Bettina, lazed about all day watching chat shows, flicking through magazines and day-dreaming of marrying professional footballers. But Belle, the youngest daughter, was a great help to her father in running his business. She also enjoyed reading books on engineering and space exploration, for she was as intelligent as she was beautiful, and she had an avid interest in rocket science.

The businessman once had to go away on an important trip for work.

"Don't forget to bring us back some jewellery!" yelled Bianca.

"And some perfume!" bellowed Bettina.

"Is there nothing you would like, darling?" the businessman asked Belle.

Belle thought for a while. "Just a beautiful rose, please Daddy," she smiled.

"That's my girl!" the businessman said, and gave a cheery wave as he drove away.

But when the businessman finally returned, he was downcast and empty-handed.

"I'm afraid your dear old Dad has had it," the

businessman explained. "I was on my way back last night, but it was dark and raining and somehow I got completely lost in the middle of nowhere. The only house for miles around was a spooky old mansion, and I went to ask for help. The lights were on, the front door was open, but nobody seemed to be at home. I thought it was very strange, but I was so desperate that I crept inside and stayed the night. Early this morning, as I was hurrying off through the grounds, I stopped to pick a rose for Belle. 'STOP THIEF!' someone roared. 'This is my house and those are my roses! Is this how you repay my hospitality? I am going to kill you!' The man who came striding towards me was uglier than a monster in a film.

He had a hairy face and bloodshot eyes, a snout for a nose and teeth like fangs. His hands were clawed and his body huge and hulking. I realised that the beast was deadly serious, so I fell on my knees in terror and begged for mercy. 'I will give you three months to say goodbye to everyone,' he growled. 'After that, you must return here to die . . . unless you have a daughter who is willing to come in your place and live here with me forever.'"

Bianca and Bettina stood gawping in horror. "Oh Daddy," they wailed, "who is going to look after us when you're gone?"

"Don't worry, Daddy," Belle comforted her father. "I can't let you die. I will go instead of you."

"Belle, you will do nothing of the kind!" her father protested. "You haven't seen this guy!"

"I don't care!" said Belle, resolutely sticking out her chin. And nothing Belle's father could say would make her change her mind. "If you sneak off without me, I shall just follow you," was her final word on the subject. So three months later, the broken-hearted businessman accompanied his brave daughter to the door of the huge, lonely mansion and kissed her for the last time. He could hardly see through his tears as he turned and walked away . . .

"Right," Belle said to herself firmly, though her bottom lip was trembling. "Let's find the library. Maybe it has a good science section." She set off through the stone corridors and oak-panelled halls, exploring. It was an eerie feeling to be all alone in such an enormous old place. Suddenly, Belle stopped in surprise. There, right in front of her was a door marked 'Belle's room'. She put her hand on the iron handle and gently pushed. It swung open with a creak. Belle gasped with delight. Inside, was everything she could possibly have wished for. There was a soft, white bed.

Wardrobes full of beautiful clothes. But best of all, lining the walls was shelf after shelf of books.

"The owner of this place can't be all bad," Belle murmured to herself. She drew down the nearest book. It was bound in ancient leather and had gold-edging. She read the first page:

Belle, you have a heart of gold
Like girls in fairytales of old.
Whatever you wish, it will come true
There's magic waiting here for you.

"Hmmm," wondered Belle. "Well, the only thing I really wish is that I could see if my Dad is okay."

At that very moment, Belle noticed a mirror on the bedroom wall begin to cloud over. Mists swirled across the glass, and when they cleared, instead of her own reflection, she saw a picture of her father, sitting at home sadly without her. After a few moments the picture vanished, but Belle was very grateful to have been able to see her father at all. The owner of this place is actually very kind, Belle thought to herself.

Just then, Belle heard the dinner bell ringing from the great hall. She hurried along and found a delicious meal laid out for one. No sooner had she swallowed three mouthfuls than she heard a shuffling and a snuffling. The food stuck in her throat and her heartbeat quickened. Belle forced herself to turn round and face her host.

Her father had been right. He was truly hideous.

"I'm Belle," she whispered, remembering her manners, like the well-brought up girl she was. "My room is wonderful – thank you."

"Call me Beast," said the monster, a look of pleasure lighting up his sad eyes. "Did you really like everything?"

"Yes, of course," said Belle. "Particularly the books. I love books, especially those on rocket science."

"They are your books now," said Beast. "Everything here is yours. I give it all to you. You can do with everything just what you wish. That goes for me, too. If I'm bothering you just tell me to go away and I will." The Beast looked down at his huge, flat feet. "I know I'm exceedingly ugly. I might put you off your food." He sighed. "And not only am I ugly, I'm very stupid too."

"Now, now," comforted Belle. "I'm sure that's not the case. Anyone who is ready to say they are stupid can't possibly be stupid. The only people who really are stupid are those who won't admit that they're stupid!"

"Do you really think so?" sighed the Beast.

"Yes, of course!" laughed Belle. "And if you're really worried about being stupid, I can teach you all about rocket science. Let me get my books . . ."

A sheepish smile came over the Beast's ugly face as he listened to Belle read. After a while, he suddenly interrupted her.

"Belle, will you marry me?" he asked.

Belle was extremely taken aback. She looked at the monster as he crouched adoringly in front of her. "I'm sorry," she said. "I wish I could, but I really don't want to."

And so the time passed. Each day, Belle read in her room and walked in the beautiful grounds, admiring the roses. And each evening, the Beast came to visit her. As the weeks went on, Belle began to enjoy his company and looked forward to seeing him. But each night the Beast asked her to marry him, and even though Belle liked him more and more as a friend, she simply couldn't – well, fancy him.

Belle's only other worry was her Dad. Each day she saw in the mirror that he was pining more and more without her. Her sisters were selfish, unkind and thoughtless, and her father had grown quiet and pale and thin.

"Dear Beast," Belle begged one night, "allow me to go back to see my dad. I am afraid that he is dying of a broken heart."

Much to Belle's surprise, the Beast nodded his agreement. "Of course, Belle," he said, "if that is what will make you happy. Only I don't know what I'll do without you ..."

"Darling Beast," whispered Belle, stroking his matted, shaggy hair, "I promise I'll be back in a week."

"Then I promise you that when you wake up tomorrow morning, you'll be at home with your father," sighed the Beast. "Take this ring. When you're ready to leave, just put it by the side of your bed at night. As you sleep, it will bring you back here."

Sure enough, next morning Belle woke up back in her old bed. Her dad couldn't believe his eyes! He and Belle hugged and laughed and spent a wonderful holiday doing all the things they used to enjoy doing together – going through his accounts, visiting the science museum, watching old musicals on TV . . . The week flew by in the twinkling of an eye. "Please, Belle, don't go," begged her dad, and Belle didn't have the heart to leave.

But several nights later, Belle had a terrible dream. She saw the Beast lying in the garden of his mansion, under the rose bushes that he loved so much. Belle knew that he was dying.

"Daddy," she sobbed the next morning.

"I'm worried that something dreadful has happened to the Beast. He's my best and truest friend – and it's all my fault!"

That night, Belle put the Beast's ring by her bedside. It didn't seem as if she'd been asleep for five minutes when she woke up in her beautiful white room in the mansion. Belle sped off into the moonlit garden and there, lying under the rose bushes just as in her dream, lay the Beast. She flung herself down by his side and heaved his big, heavy head into her lap. Her tears plopped one by one onto his hairy face.

Weakly, the Beast opened his eyes and smiled. "I thought you had forgotten your promise," he whispered. "Now I have seen you once again, I can die happily."

"No!" Belle cried. "You can't die! You mustn't leave me! I love you!" And she kissed him.

At that very moment, the night sky was lit up by a

million rainbow-coloured fireworks. Belle gazed upwards in surprise – she thought things like that only happened in films. When she looked back down at the Beast again, the monster was gone. Lying in her lap was a handsome, happy prince. He sprang up and lifted Belle to her feet with joy in his eyes.

"My darling Belle," he told her, "Thank you for setting me free! I have lived under a wicked enchantment for years which forced me to appear as the Beast – not only ugly but stupid, too – until a beautiful girl willingly fell in love with me. You are the only person in the world who saw through my ugly appearance and sensed what I was really like inside. Now we will live together happily forever."

And that's exactly what they did. But this is a real tale, not a fairytale, and real tales don't have entirely happy endings. The prince took Belle to live at his palace –

and her dad went to live with them too. But Belle's selfish sisters got what they deserved. They were turned into statues and set at the palace gates until such time as they began to think about other people rather than themselves. As far as I know, they're both there still . . .

Pandora's Box

a Greek myth

When the world was first created, it was a happy place of light and laughter; there was no such thing as sadness or pain. The sun shone every day and the gods came down from heaven to walk and talk with the humans who lived on earth.

One afternoon, a man called Epimetheus and his wife, Pandora, were outside tending their flower garden when they saw the god Mercury approaching. He was bowed down by a dark wooden chest that he was carrying on his shoulders and he looked hot and tired. Pandora rushed to get the worn-out god a cool drink, while

Epimetheus helped him lower the chest onto the ground. It was tied shut with golden cords and was carved with strange markings.

"My friends, would you do me a great favour?" sighed Mercury. "It is so hot today and the box is so heavy! May I leave it here while I go on an errand?"

"Of course you can," smiled Epimetheus.

The man and the god heaved the chest indoors.

"Are you sure that no one will find it?" asked Mercury anxiously. "NO ONE under ANY circumstances must open the box."

"Don't worry," laughed Epimetheus and Pandora, and they waved the god off through the trees.

All of a sudden, Pandora stopped still and frowned. "Listen, Epimetheus!" she hissed. "I am sure I heard someone whispering our names!"

Epimetheus and Pandora listened hard. At first, they

heard nothing but the twittering of the birds in the
sunshine and the rustling of the leaves in the breeze. Then,
they heard the distant sound of "Epimetheus! Pandora!"
being called from outside.

"It's our friends!" cried Epimetheus, happily.

But Pandora looked puzzled and shook her head.
"No, Epimetheus, those aren't the voices I heard,"
she said, firmly.

"They must have been!" Epimetheus laughed.
"Come on now, let's go and see everyone."

"You go," Pandora insisted, with a frown. "I'd rather
stay here for a while."

Epimetheus shrugged, kissed Pandora on the nose,
and strode outside. As soon as he was gone, Pandora
hurried over to the strange box and waited. After only a
few seconds, she heard it again – distant voices calling
"Pandora! Pandora!" The voices were so low and whispery

that Pandora wasn't sure whether she really was hearing them or was just imagining it.. She bent down closer and put her ear to the lid. No, this time she was sure. The box was calling to her! "Pandora!" the voices pleaded. "Let us out, Pandora! We are trapped in here in the darkness! Please help us to escape!"

Pandora jumped back with a start. Mercury had expressly forbade them or anyone else to open the box . . . and yet the voices sounded so sad and pitiful.

"Pandora!" they came again. "Help us! Help us, we beg you!"

Pandora could stand it no longer. Hurriedly, she knelt down and worked at the tight golden knots. All the time, the whispering and pleading voices filled her ears.

At last the knots were undone and the gleaming cords fell away. She took a deep breath and opened the lid.

At once, Pandora realised she had done a terrible thing. The box had been crammed with all the evils in the world – thousands of tiny, brown, moth-like creatures that stung people with their wings and caused hurt and misery wherever they went. Now, thanks to Pandora, the evils were free! They flew up out of the chest in a great swarm and fluttered all over Pandora's skin. For the very first time, Pandora felt pain and regret. She began to wail with despair, and all too late, she slammed the lid back down onto the box.

Outside, Epimetheus heard his wife's cries and came running as fast as he could. The little creatures fluttered to sting and bite him, before speeding off through the window into the world beyond. For the first time ever, Epimetheus began to shout at his wife in anger. Pandora yelled back, and the couple realised in horror that they were arguing.

"Let me out!" interrupted a high voice. Pandora and Epimetheus grabbed onto each other in a panic. The voice was coming from inside the box. "Don't be afraid of me! Let me out and I can help you!" came the voice.

"What do you think?" Pandora whispered to Epimetheus, wide-eyed.

"Surely you can't do any more mischief than you already have done," he grumbled. So Pandora shut her eyes and opened Mercury's chest for a second time.

Out of the deep, dark box fluttered a single shining white spirit like a butterfly. It was Hope. Pandora and Epimetheus sobbed with relief as she fluttered against their skin and soothed their stinging wounds. Then she was gone, darting out of the window and into the world after the evils. And luckily, Hope has stayed with us ever since.

Tomlin

a Scottish folk tale

Carterhaugh Wood was thick and green and dark, and people said it was the home of fairy folk. One bright summer's day, Janet, the earl's daughter, made up her mind to go and explore it for herself. She crept out of the castle and set off down a narrow path deep into the woods. After a while, Janet reached a small stone well in the middle of a clearing. There were roses climbing all over it – far more beautiful than any in the castle gardens – and Janet bent to pick one. No sooner had the stem broken off in her hand than Janet heard a voice that said, "Naughty-naughty, Janet.

Who said you could come here into our wood and pick one of our roses?"

Janet straightened up with a start. There before her stood the most handsome young knight she had ever seen. She tossed her hair proudly and replied, "How dare you speak to me like that! These woods belong to my father, the earl. I shall go where I choose and pick whatever flowers I like!"

Delight sparkled in the young man's eyes at her bold answer and he threw back his head and laughed. "I am Tomlin," the knight said, taking Janet's hands and spinning her round, "and today you shall stay here in the forest with me and we shall play."

All day long, Tomlin and Janet wandered through Carterhaugh Wood. They danced and sang and told each other stories. And by the evening, they were deeply in love.

"I will not return to the castle without you," Janet

vowed. "You must come with me and I will beg my father to let you stay."

"I cannot leave the wood," replied Tomlin sadly. "I was once human, but many years ago, when I was riding through the forest, the Fairy Queen caught me and enchanted me. Now I am an elf-knight, and I must ride by the side of the Fairy Queen to protect her for ever more. I only wish that I could be a man again, for then I would surely marry you."

"Is there no way to break the spell?" Janet sighed.

"There is," Tomlin said gently, "but you must be very brave."

"Tell me what I must do," Janet whispered.

"This very night is Halloween," Tomlin explained, "a night when fairies, goblins and witches ride abroad. You must go to Mile Cross and hide there until midnight, for then I will come riding by. First you will see a troop of riders on black horses. Then there will be a troop on brown horses. Next will come riders on horses as white as milk – and in the middle of them will ride the Fairy Queen herself. I will be among the elf-knights at her side, and I will wear only one glove so you can find me quickly among the throng. When you see me, you must run to my horse, seize its bridle and drag me down. You must then hold me fast, no matter what happens – for the fairy folk will cast all sorts of spells on me to try to keep me. If you have the strength and courage not to let go, the

enchantment will at last be broken and I will be yours."
Tomlin took Janet's hand. "Do you think you can do all
this?" he asked quietly.

"Yes," breathed Janet. "Yes, I will."

Later that night, when everyone else was safely
inside the castle with the doors and windows barred, Janet
hid in the darkness on the moor at Mile Cross. Just before
the stroke of midnight, she heard the thunder of hooves
and out of the night appeared hundreds of black horses,
bridles jangling and manes flying. On their backs were
witches with bony fingers and sunken faces with dead,
staring eyes.

Next, the brown horses galloped past, whinnying
and snorting. The wrinkled goblins who rode them
whipped them with willow switches and clutched the reins
with wizened fingers.

Then the white horses came like glowing ghosts

through the gloom, wild-eyed and foaming at the mouth, and at the centre of the riders Janet saw the beautiful Fairy Queen, sitting tall and fierce and proud. Quickly, Janet searched for a rider with only one glove. She plunged in among the pounding hooves, pulled down the enchanted elf-knight and held Tomlin to herself as tight as she could.

The Fairy Queen sent up an unearthly wail that tore through the darkness and all the hundreds of riders thundered around, shrieking and howling. Suddenly Janet felt Tomlin grow in her arms and she realised she was holding a huge, hairy bear. Still she held him fast, and he writhed into a hissing snake. Still she clutched him in her arms, and he bucked into an angry, snapping wolf. Still she held on tight, and he turned into a blazing branch that

burnt into her flesh. Still Janet refused to let go, and in a
flash of cold lightning she saw she was at last holding a
naked, human man. As she wrapped Tomlin in her cloak, a
haunting cry came from the Fairy Queen: "Tomlin, I
would rather have changed your eyes to wood and your
heart to stone than lost you!" Then suddenly the wild hunt
was gone, disappeared into the night, and Janet and Tomlin
were left alone on the dark, windy moor to make their
way home to the castle together.

Hop-Toads and Pearls

a retelling from the original tale by Charles Perrault

G o and fetch the water!" yelled the widow at her younger daughter. "You can finish that sweeping later! And hurry back with it. You've still got to light the fire and peel the potatoes for dinner."

The poor girl hurried to rest her broom in the corner and wipe her dusty hands on her tattered apron. She never grumbled about being treated like a slave because she was good and kind and couldn't think badly about anybody. But how she wished that her mother and her sister might help her out a little with all the housework now and again . . .

As the exhausted girl stumbled out to the well with the cumbersome bucket, the widow's elder daughter looked up from her comfy chair by the window and smirked. Fanchon was like her mother in every way: how she looked (very ugly), how she spoke (sharp and nasty) and how she acted (selfish and lazy). This was the reason why her mother adored her so: whenever she looked at Fanchon, she saw herself.

The widow's younger daughter reached the well and heaved up a heavy, full bucket. Suddenly, she noticed that an old beggar-woman had joined her. The toothless crone wheezed, "My dear, I'm hoarse with thirst. Could you spare me a little drink?"

"Of course," the girl said, and hurried to unhook the dripping bucket and help the beggar-woman to a ladleful.

Little did the younger daughter know that the hag who stood in front of her was actually a powerful fairy, who had disguised herself to put the girl to the test. The younger daughter kindly helped the beggar-woman to another ladleful of water and chatted politely to her for a while, before hauling the bucket back home.

How the girl's mother and her sister yelled and screamed and swore at her for taking so long at the well! "I do beg your pardon," the poor girl apologised. "I will be quicker next time." To everyone's surprise, a shining white pearl dropped from her lips with every word.

The stunned widow woman picked up a pearl from the floor, bit it hard between her teeth, and held it up to the light to examine it. "They're real!" she exclaimed, with a greedy twinkle in her eye. "What on earth happened at the well this evening? Tell me everything, or I'll lock you in the coal cellar all weekend."

The younger daughter was just as amazed as her mother and sister, and truthfully told them that she had done nothing but give a drink to a woman she'd met at the well. Pearls continued to drop from her lips as she spoke, and as fast as they fell, the widow scooped them up greedily into her pockets.

"Did you hear that, Fanchon?" she screeched delightedly. "Get yourself down to that well immediately!"

"Get lost!" the rude girl snorted. "I'm not fetching and carrying like a slave for anything!"

"I said GO!" the widow roared, cuffing the horrified Fanchon round the head. "Find that woman and give her a drink, whether she wants one or not! We're going to be rich, rich, rich! . . ."

Fanchon sulked and pouted, grumbled and cursed with every step that she lugged the splintery bucket – and it was only fear of her mother's temper that made her do it at all. She flung the bucket angrily into the well and moaned and groaned to herself with every wind as she pulled it back up. No sooner had she finished, than she noticed she had been joined by an elegant young woman dressed in fine robes. (It was the fairy again, but this time she had disguised herself as a princess.) "Good evening," the princess said politely, "would you be so good as to allow me a drink?"

"Oh, it's you, is it?" Fanchon sneered. "You're the reason I've got splinters in my hands, splashes all over my dress, and my arms are killing me. You'd better make it worth my while and give me diamonds instead of pearls, that's all I can say." With that, Fanchon angrily flung the wooden ladle at the princess and dumped the bucket at her feet. "Go on then," she snapped.

No sooner had the princess taken one sip than Fanchon snatched the ladle back and humped the bucket back to the house. "There!" she yelled at her mother. "Happy now?" To everyone's horror, three great hop-toads leapt from her lips and sprang across the floor, croaking. Fanchon clapped her hands over her mouth in alarm.

"Whatever's happened?" cried the widow. "Where are the pearls?"

"I don't know!" wailed Fanchon, and three more hop-toads bounced, bulging-eyed, from her mouth. She began to scream and stamp her feet.

"This is all your fault, you ungrateful wretch!" the widow yelled at her younger daughter. She shoved the girl outside and slammed the door in her face. The poor younger daughter wandered off into the forest, sobbing . . .

The girl would almost certainly have got lost in the woods forever if the prince hadn't spotted her on his way back from a hunting trip. The prince was fascinated by the pearls that fell from her mouth, but he was even more charmed by the forgiving, kind way in which she spoke of her obviously horrible family. He took the lovely girl back to his palace at once, and after she had got to know and love him, he married her.

As for the nasty elder daughter, well, even her own mother tired of her moaning in the end. Besides, who wants to live with a house full of hop-toads? The widow threw the girl out, and they both lived the rest of their lives with only their miserable selves for company.

Firebird

a Russian fairytale

L ong ago in Russia, in the days when witches lurked in the forests and dragons flew over the plains and demons hid in the mountains, there lived a lord called Tsar Andronovich who owned a magnificent garden. At the centre of the garden lay a beautiful orchard, and in the middle of the orchard lay Tsar Andronovich's favourite tree – a tree which grew precious golden apples. Tsar Andronovich had given strict orders that no one was allowed to touch the golden apple tree except for himself. But one night, an amazing firebird with wings of flame and eyes of crystal came blazing into the orchard and stole some of the precious fruit.

"I must have this amazing firebird alive!" Tsar Andronovich marvelled. "This creature seems even more splendid than the golden apples she has been stealing!"

Half an hour later, the Tsar's three sons were galloping out of the gates in search of the firebird. The eldest and middle son, Dimitri and Vassili, thundered off together. They had teamed up to find the firebird and agreed to split their father's fortune between them. The youngest son, Ivan, was left to go off sadly on his own.

Ivan rode for three days and nights without any idea of where he was going and without seeing any sign of the firebird. His food and water began to run low and his horse was exhausted. Just as Ivan was thinking things couldn't get much worse, he heard a blood-curdling howl behind him and out of a dark forest ran a huge grey wolf. Ivan's horse shot away from under him, throwing him into the dirt. But it didn't escape very far. The grey wolf sprang onto it and gobbled it up.

"Eat me quickly and have done with it!" Ivan cried at the panting beast.

"I am not going to eat you," grinned the wolf. "I have to repay you for eating your very tasty horse! Now, I can't help noticing that you look worn out. Ride on me, the grey wolf. I will take you where you want to go."

Ivan was too tired and lonely to argue. He climbed onto the grey wolf's back and explained all about his quest to find the firebird. He had hardly finished speaking when the grey wolf leapt away like an arrow. It seemed like only a few seconds before they came to a halt before a stone wall.

"Ivan, climb over this wall and you will see the firebird in a golden cage," the wolf explained. "Take the firebird, but whatever you do, do not steal the golden cage."

Trembling, Ivan clambered over the wall and found himself in a courtyard below. Hanging from a tree in the middle was a golden cage with the firebird inside, just as the wolf had said. Ivan crept up to the leafy boughs, opened the jewelled door, and drew out the beautiful firebird. To his great surprise, she didn't flap or cry out or make any fuss at all. Hmmm, thought Ivan to himself. I really need the cage as well, or else where am I going to keep the firebird? He reached up into the leaves and unhooked the cage. At that very moment, ear-splitting alarm bells began to ring and guards rushed into the courtyard from all sides. They roughly dragged Ivan off to see their master, the Tsar Dolmat.

"You must pay dearly for trying to steal my precious firebird," boomed Tsar Dolmat, his face dark with anger. Then he rubbed his beard and thought for a second. "UNLESS," he added, "you go to the ends of the earth and bring me the horse with the golden mane. If you can do this, I will give you the firebird with pleasure."

Ivan crept back to the grey wolf hanging his head in shame. But his friend simply said, "Ride on me, the grey wolf, and I will take you where you want to go."

The grey wolf sprang away to the ends of the earth faster than the wind. It seemed like only a couple of minutes before they came to a stop outside some stables.

"Ivan, go into these stables and take the horse with the golden mane," the wolf told him. "But whatever you do, do not steal its golden bridle."

Cautiously, Ivan edged into the stables, crept up to the horse with the golden mane, and began to lead it out of its stall. Hmmm, thought Ivan, as he looked at its golden bridle hanging on the wall. I really need the bridle as well, or else how am I going to ride the horse? The moment he lifted down the bridle a clanging peal of bells broke the silence. Soldiers dashed into the stable and hauled Ivan away to see their master, the Tsar Afron.

"You must pay dearly for trying to steal my wonderful horse with the golden mane," raged Tsar Afron, shaking with fury. "UNLESS," he added, "you go to the other side of the world and bring me Tasha the Beautiful to be my bride. If you can do this, I will gladly give you the horse with the golden mane."

Ivan could hardly bring himself to tell the grey wolf that he had disobeyed him a second time. But when the wolf saw Ivan returning empty-handed he simply said, "Ride on me, the grey wolf, and I will take you where you want to go."

Ivan jumped onto the grey wolf and he sped away to the other side of the world as quick as lightning. It seemed like only an hour or so before they drew up outside a glorious palace.

"Ivan, this time I am going to be the one who goes inside and you are going to be the one who waits," said the wolf and he sprang over the palace wall with one mighty bound. Ivan hardly had time to draw breath before the wolf came over again – this time with Tasha the Beautiful tossed onto his back. Ivan leapt onto the wolf's back and they were off through the air like a shooting star.

By the time the three arrived back at Tsar Afron's

home, the grey wolf was highly
surprised to find Ivan
weeping bitterly.

"Why are you
crying?" the grey wolf
asked. "If we give Tasha
the Beautiful to Tsar Afron,
you will get the horse with the

golden mane. If we give the horse with the golden mane to
Tsar Dolmat, you will get the firebird. If we give the
firebird to Tsar Andronovich, your father, you will get all
the wealth he possesses."

"But I have fallen in love with Tasha," Ivan
protested, "and she has fallen in love with me!"

The grey wolf looked at Tasha the Beautiful and she
nodded sadly, biting her lip.

"Oh very well," sighed the grey wolf. "I will turn

myself into the form of Tasha the Beautiful. You can present me to Tsar Afron in her place and he will give you the horse with the golden mane. When you are safely two mountains away, think of me, the grey wolf, and I will be back at your side."

And so it all happened. Tsar Afron was tricked and soon Ivan was once again mounted on the grey wolf while his sweetheart Tasha the Beautiful rode prettily on the horse with the golden mane.

As they drew near the villa of Tsar Dolmat, Ivan sighed a deep sigh. "Oh grey wolf," he began, "I would so like to keep this horse with a golden mane. Would you turn into the form of the horse, as you disguised yourself as Tasha before? Then I could take you to Tsar Dolmat and win the firebird. When I am safely two forests away, I will think of you and you will return back to my side."

The grey wolf looked at Ivan and bowed slightly.

"For you, I will do this," said the wolf gruffly. And so it all came to pass. Tsar Dolmat was tricked, and Ivan was once again mounted on the grey wolf while his sweetheart Tasha the Beautiful rode prettily on the horse with the golden mane and carried the firebird.

By and by, the companions came to the very spot where the grey wolf had set upon Ivan's horse and eaten it. Then it was the grey wolf's turn to sigh a deep sigh. "Well, Ivan, here I took a horse from you and here I now return you with another horse – and a beautiful bride and a firebird, too! You no longer need me and I must go!" And the wolf loped off into the woods and was gone.

Ivan and Tasha went on their way in sadness, weeping for their lost friend. When they were very nearly back home at Tsar Andronovich's house, they stopped to rest and sank into an exhausted sleep. Even the firebird was so soundly asleep that she didn't notice two figures come creeping out of the shadows. It was Dimitri and Vassily, who had returned from their travels empty handed and were enraged to find their little brother not only with the firebird but also with Tasha the Beautiful! In their bitterness, the brothers drew their swords and stabbed Ivan where he lay dreaming. Then they swept up Tasha the Beautiful and the firebird and were off to their father's mansion, to pretend that the treasures were theirs. "Breathe a word of this and we'll kill you," they hissed into Tasha's ear, and Tasha shook with sorrow and fear . . .

Ivan's body lay lifeless and cold as snow started to cover him like a thick blanket. A few bold birds and woodland creatures began to creep closer to find out what type of thing would lie so silent and still in the freezing weather – and among them came a grey wolf with yellow eyes and drooling jaws. He stalked right up to Ivan's body and sniffed all round. Then he sat in the snow, threw his

head back and howled a spine-chilling howl. Slowly and gently the wolf began to lick the wound in Ivan's chest. And suddenly, Ivan sat up and began to shiver. "What am I doing asleep in this snowstorm?" he asked the grey wolf.

"Ride on me, the grey wolf," came the gruff voice, "and I will take you where you want to go."

"Home," whispered Ivan into his friend's ear, "I want to go home." And no sooner had he finished saying the words than they were there.

Of course, when Tsar Andronovich learnt the truth, he threw the wicked Dimitri and Vassily in a dungeon, where they belonged. Ivan and Tasha the Beautiful were married – Ivan rode his faithful grey wolf to the wedding ceremony and Tasha arrived on the horse with the golden mane. As for Tsar Andronovich, well he got his precious firebird after all – and he loved her so much he even let her eat the golden apples from his favourite tree whenever she wanted.

The Red Shoes

retold from the original tale by Hans Christian Andersen

There was once a woman who was so poor that she couldn't afford to buy her daughter, Karen, any shoes. The woman often wept to see Karen's feet all rough and blistered. She would have been overjoyed to know that the shoemaker's wife felt so sorry for Karen that she was making her a pair of red shoes from some of her husband's left-over leather. But the woman never found out. She died the very day that the red shoes were finished and Karen wore them for the first time as she walked behind her mother's coffin on the way to church.

The shoemaker's wife couldn't sew very well and the

shoes had turned out to be rather clumsy and misshapen. But Karen thought that her soft, red shoes were the most wonderful things in all the world. However, the old lady who kindly took Karen in said, "You can't possibly go walking around in those odd things. Whatever will people think?" She threw the red shoes onto the fire and bought Karen a pair of sensible, sturdy black ones.

It was the sensible, sturdy black shoes that Karen was wearing when the old lady took her to the palace to see the parade for the little princess's birthday. The king and queen stood with the little princess on the balcony, waving and smiling. But Karen didn't look at the gracious expressions on their faces, or their fine rich robes. Karen couldn't take her eyes off the red shoes on the little princess's feet. They were magnificent – made out of satin instead of leather, so they actually shone like rubies. Those really are the most wonderful things in all the world, thought Karen.

From that moment, whenever Karen buckled on her sensible, black shoes, she thought of the little princess's beautiful red ones. Whenever Karen took off her sensible black shoes, she thought of the princess's beautiful red ones. And she longed for those beautiful red shoes with all her heart.

One day, the old lady who looked after Karen looked at her sensible,black shoes and tutted, "My, my! Those are looking rather old and shabby – and they're too small for you now. We can't have you going along to church in those tomorrow." The old lady handed her a purse full of money. "Buy yourself some new ones," she smiled.

Karen walked all the way to the shoe shop with a thumping heart. First, she tried on some sensible, sturdy black shoes – but there were none to fit her. Then she tried on some smart, lace-up brown shoes – but they still either slopped up and down or cramped her toes. Then Karen peered up at a high shelf and saw a red pair exactly like the ones the little princess had worn. They fitted her perfectly. Karen held her breath as she handed over her money and stepped out of the shop. Her feet gleamed and twinkled in the sunlight. She could hardly believe it. Her dream had come true.

Karen knew full well that the old lady wouldn't approve at all of her choice. But luckily for her, the old lady's eyesight wasn't what it was, and the colour of

Karen's new shoes was just a dark blur. Karen kept quiet, saying nothing of the truth.

Next day, Karen's heart nearly burst with excitement as she slipped on her red shoes. She tripped gaily all the way to church, and even though it was a beautiful day and there were many finely dressed people about, she had eyes for no one and nothing except the red shoes. She twisted and turned as she walked, so her toes and heels shone in turn. She hoped that everyone would see them.

Even when Karen was sitting in her church pew, she couldn't take her eyes off her red shoes. Even when the priest was praying,

she couldn't take her eyes off her red shoes. Even when the organist began to strike up a joyful hymn of praise, she couldn't take her eyes off the red shoes. The statues of the angels and saints seemed to frown down sternly upon her, but Karen didn't notice. She still couldn't take her eyes off the red shoes.

As the choir started to sing out and their voices filled the air, Karen felt a strange sensation in her feet. Her toes began to twitch inside the red satin. Her heels began to quiver to and fro. Suddenly, Karen's feet began to dance. Right there and then in church, Karen's red shoes forced her to stand up and leap and turn and skip. With the eyes of the whole congregation staring at her, Karen's red shoes danced her down the aisle and out into the sunlight. "Help me!" she cried, but no one knew what to do. The red shoes danced Karen all around the graveyard and out of the church gate. Then they danced her round and round the churchyard wall and off down the street . . .

By day and by night, the enchanted red shoes carried Karen along, twinkling wickedly. They danced her in and out of houses and up and down stairs. They danced her right through the city gates across the fields and into the dark forest. They danced her out of the trees and through meadows, until Karen had quite forgotten how long she had been dancing . . . and still they made Karen dance. "Forgive me!" the sobbing girl cried out. "Forgive me for thinking of these foolish pretty things above everything else!" At last, the red shoes were still. Utterly exhausted, Karen collapsed into a heap and closed her eyes. And when her soul reached heaven, she never had to dance or think about red shoes ever again.

The Magic Tinderbox

retold from the original tale by Hans Christian Andersen

A soldier came marching down the road – left, right! left, right! left, right! "Good morning, sir," croaked an ugly witch sitting at the roadside. "If you do as I say, I will make you very rich. You see that huge tree there –" the witch pointed over to an old oak – "it is quite hollow." You must climb to the top, wriggle through a hole and then lower yourself down the inside of the trunk all the way to the bottom. You will see three doors. Open the first one and you will find yourself inside a room where a frightening dog sits on a box full of money. Spread my blue-and-white checked apron on the floor, put the dog onto it, and he won't bother you at all. Then you can open the box and take out as much money as you can carry. In this first room, the money will be copper. If you'd rather have silver, you must face the even scarier dog in the second room. If you'd prefer gold, you must go into the third room – but there the dog is yet more terrifying."

"What do you want for yourself?" the soldier grinned.

"I don't want a single coin of the money," the witch cackled. "Just bring me a rusty old tinderbox that my granny forgot last time she was in there."

"Very well," agreed the soldier, and the witch gave him her apron. Then the soldier shimmied up the outside of the old oak tree, wriggled through the hole, and lowered himself down . . . down . . . down the inside. He found

himself in a long corridor lit by one hundred burning
lanterns, and sure enough, there were three doors in front
of him. The soldier bravely put his hand on the first
doorknob and turned it.

"Great Scott!" he cried, springing
back in alarm. There in the middle of the
room was a dog with eyes the size of
teacups. The soldier tore his eyes away
from its staring gaze, lay the witch's
apron on the floor and lifted the dog on
to it. Then he unlocked the box the dog
had been sitting on. Amazing! It was
filled to the brim with shining copper
coins. The soldier gleefully grabbed huge
handfuls and stuffed them into his knapsa
his pockets and even his boots.

The second dog couldn't possibly have eyes bigger

than that first one, the soldier thought to himself. Boldly, he walked to the second doorknob and turned it . . .

"Good lord!" he yelled. There in the middle of the room was a dog with eyes the size of mill-wheels. Round and round and round they churned – it made you dizzy just to look at them. Once again, the soldier forced himself to look away. He laid the witch's apron down, heaved the dog onto it, and unlocked the box on which it had been sitting. Fantastic! There before him was a treasure trove of silver! The soldier got rid of all the copper coins quick as quick and filled his knapsack, pockets and boots.

"Surely the third dog's eyes can't be any bigger than that!" the soldier said to himself, laughing at his good luck. He went to the third doorknob and turned it . . .

"Heavens above!" he cried. The third dog had eyes the size of the Round Tower of the city of Copenhagen. Not only that, but they whizzed round and round in his head like Catherine Wheels. It was several minutes before the soldier found he could look at something other than the dog's enormous spinning eyeballs. Then he laid down the witch's apron, hauled the dog onto it, and unlocked the box it had been sitting on. Unbelievable! There was enough gold to buy the palace of the King of Denmark himself! Chortling with joy, the soldier emptied his knapsack, pockets and boots of every last silver coin and crammed them with gold instead. He hurried off down the corridor, found the tinderbox, and then climbed up . . . up . . . up and out of the tree.

"Where's my tinderbox then?" the witch cackled.

"Tell me why you want it so badly and I'll give it to you," replied the soldier, firmly.

"Where IS IT?" the witch shrieked in annoyance.

"If you don't tell me why you want it, I'll cut off your head," insisted the soldier.

"GIVE ME MY TINDERBOX!" the witch howled in frustration.

"Very well," said the soldier, and he drew his sword and cut off the witch's head. Then he went on his merry way down the road, with his knapsack, pockets and boots weighed down with gold, and the witch's tinderbox tucked safely inside his jacket.

At the very next town, the soldier booked into the best hotel, ate in the most expensive restaurant, and went to the most exclusive shop to buy himself new clothes. At once the soldier found he had a lot of new friends and

they told him of all the wonders to be seen in the town – particularly the beautiful princess, who lived in the castle on top of the hill.

"How can I get to see this princess?"
the soldier asked.

"You can't," his new friends explained, "no one can.
For it has been prophesied that she will one day marry a
common soldier, and the king and queen keep the princess
locked up so this can never happen."

Day after day, the soldier spent his gold on the finest
things money could buy for himself and his friends. It was
a horrible shock when he went one morning to fill his
pockets and found that all the gold was gone. Suddenly,
the soldier's friends disappeared. The soldier had to move
out of the grand hotel and into a dingy attic at the top of
fourteen flights of stairs. He didn't even have enough
money for a candle to cheer things up with a bit of light.
Then the soldier remembered the witch's tinderbox. Surely
he could use that to give him a few sparks to start a

warming fire? No sooner had the soldier struck the tinderbox once with the flint than there was a flash of lightning and the dog with eyes the size of teacups appeared.

"What is your command, sir?" the dog growled, bowing its head respectfully.

Once the soldier had got over the shock, he stammered, "Well, I suppose I'd really like you to get me some money."

The dog immediately vanished – but reappeared an instant later with a purse of money clamped between its jaws.

The soldier whooped and danced about with delight. Suddenly he understood the secret of the tinderbox. Strike it once, twice or three times, and the dog from the first, second or third room appeared to grant his wishes!

Soon the soldier was richer than ever. He moved back into the grand hotel, ate at the expensive restaurant once again, bought himself new suits of fine clothes, and found himself surrounded by friends once more. He had everything he could wish for – except for a wife to share it all with. That princess must be very bored locked up there in the castle, the soldier thought to himself.

The soldier waited till it was dark, then struck the tinderbox once. In a flash, the dog with the eyes like teacups appeared. "I would like to see the beautiful princess," the soldier said. Before he could blink, the dog ran off and then reappeared with the princess lying on its broad back, fast asleep. She was indeed very beautiful and the soldier couldn't resist bending over to give her a kiss. The dog then disappeared and the princess was gone.

Next morning, up in the castle on the hill, the princess remembered what had happened as if it had been a strange dream, and she told her mother and father all about it. The king and queen were deeply worried. The clever queen sewed a pretty silk bag, filled it with flour and tied it around her daughter's neck when she went to bed. Then the queen pierced a tiny hole in the bag, tucked the princess in and kissed her goodnight.

Of course, the soldier had fallen deeply in love with the princess and that night he sent the dog to fetch her again. Neither the dog nor the soldier noticed the thin line of flour that ran down from the silk bag and left a tell-tale trail all the way from the castle to his door. And in the morning, when the princess was safely back in her bed, the soldier was woken by royal officers breaking down his door. They grabbed him and dragged him away to be hanged.

A huge crowd of townspeople had gathered to watch the soldier die, and opposite the gallows sat the smug king and queen and all the members of the town council. Just as the hangman put the noose around the soldier's neck, the desperate man had an idea. "Will you grant me one last wish?" he yelled out to the king. "I would like to smoke a pipe of tobacco before I die."

The king thought for a moment. He didn't want to seem merciless in front of all the people, so, "Very well," he said. To the soldier's great delight, the hangman untied his hands and offered him a pipe and some matches.

"Don't worry," the soldier grinned, "I have my own light," and he pulled out his tinderbox and struck it three times.

At once, the dog with the eyes as big as teacups, the dog with the eyes as big as mill-wheels, and the dog with the eyes as big as the Round Tower of the city of Copenhagen stood before him. "Save me," the soldier cried, "or I will surely die!" The dogs growled like rumbling thunder and sprang among the crowd, scattering them everywhere in terror. They made straight for the king and queen and the table of town councillors. One by one, the dogs picked them up in their jaws and hurled them far, far away over the most distant hills. "Hooray!" the townspeople cried. "We never liked them anyway. We'd much prefer the brave soldier to be our king and the beautiful princess to be our queen!" And that's exactly what happened. They were married straight away – and the three dogs were guests of honour at the wedding feast.

Animals Big and Small

The Lion and the Mouse

a retelling from Aesop's Fables

The lion was very hungry. As he padded through the tall grass, something rustled by his feet. He reached out a great paw, and there was a squeak. He had caught a tiny mouse by the tail.

"Oh please let me go, dear lion," cried the tiny mouse. "I should be no more than a single mouthful for you. And I promise I will be able to help you some day."

The lion roared with laughter. The thought of a tiny mouse being able to help such a huge creature as himself amused him so much that he did let the mouse go.

"He would not have made much of a meal anyway," smiled the lion.

The mouse scuttled away, calling out to the lion, "I shall not forget my promise!"

Many days and nights later the lion was padding through the tall grass again when he suddenly fell into a deep pit. A net was flung over him, and he lay there helpless, caught by some hunters. He twisted and turned but he could not free himself. The hunters just laughed at his struggles and went off to fetch a cart to carry the great lion back to their village.

As he lay there, the lion heard a tiny voice.

"I promised you I would be able to help you one day."

It was the tiny mouse! And straight away he began to gnaw through the rope that held the lion fast. He gnawed and chewed, and chewed and gnawed, and eventually he chewed and gnawed right through the rope and the lion was free. With a great bound, he leapt out of the pit and then reached back, very gently, to lift the tiny mouse out too.

"I shall never forget you, mouse. Thank you for remembering your promise and saving me," purred the great lion.

So the tiny mouse was able to help the great lion. One good turn deserves another, you see?

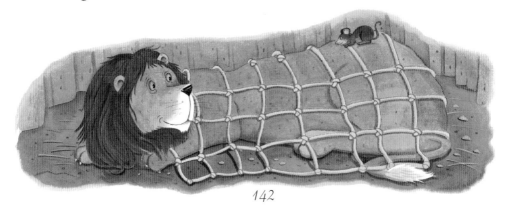

Why the Manx Cat has no Tail

a myth from the Isle of Man

The rain was falling in torrents, and there were great storm clouds building up. The rivers were overflowing and the fields looked like lakes. Noah decided that the time had come to fill his ark as planned with two of every animal that lived. He called his sons Shem and Ham and Japeth and they began rounding up the animals and leading them gently onto the ark. First came the big beasts, the giraffes and lions and elephants. Then came the cows and the sheep and the pigs. Then came the foxes and the rabbits, but not together of course. Then came the birds and the grasshoppers and the ants, who were rather nervous of the elephants' feet. Finally

came the dogs, but only one cat, a big ginger tom cat.

The she-cat, who was a stripy tabby, had decided that she

would like to go mousing one last time,

as she realised she would not be able to eat a fellow

passenger when they were all cooped up in the ark.

Mrs Noah called and called her, but still she did

not come. Cats are always contrary and she was no

exception. Noah looked at the rising water and told

Mrs Noah that he would have to pull up the gangplank as the ark would soon be afloat. All the other animals were settling in to their various stalls, and what a noise there was! Roaring and mooing, trumpeting and baaing, snorting and squawking. Toes and flippers and trotters and paws got stood on, fur and feathers were ruffled and horns and long tails got stuck, but eventually everyone was in place.

145

Noah began to pull the great door of the ark to, and just as he was about to shut it fast, up pranced the she-cat, soaking wet but licking her lips. She managed to slip through the gap in the nick of time but her great plume of a tail was caught in the door as it slammed shut. She turned round and her entire tail was cut off! The cat was very cross, but Noah told her it was entirely her own fault and she would have to wait until they found land again before she could have her tail mended.

Forty days and forty nights later, the flood was over and Noah opened the great door of the ark once more. First out was the she-cat, and she ran and ran until she found the Isle of Man, and there she stopped, too ashamed for anyone else to see her. Ever since then the cats from the Isle of Man have had no tails. Nowadays they are rather proud to be different.

Chicken Licken

an English folk tale

One fine day Chicken Licken went for a walk in the woods. Now Chicken Licken was not very bright, and he was also rather inclined to act first and think after. So when an acorn fell on his head, he decided immediately that the sky must be falling in. He set off as fast as he could to tell the king. On the way he met Henny Penny and Cocky Locky.

"I am off to tell the king that the sky is falling in," he clucked importantly.

"We will come too," said Henny Penny and Cocky Locky.

So Chicken Licken, Henny Penny and Cocky Locky set off to find the King. On the way they met Ducky Lucky and Drakey Lakey.

"We are off to tell the king that the sky is falling in," clucked Chicken Licken importantly.

"We will come too," said Ducky Lucky and Drakey Lakey.

So Chicken Licken, Henny Penny, Cocky Locky, Ducky Lucky and Drakey Lakey all set off to find the king. On the way they met Goosey Loosey and Turkey Lurkey.

"We are off to tell the king that the sky is falling in," clucked Chicken Licken importantly.

"We will come too," said Goosey Loosey and Turkey Lurkey.

So Chicken Licken, Henny Penny, Cocky Locky, Ducky Lucky, Drakey Lakey, Goosey Loosey and Turkey

Lurkey all set off to find the king. On the way they met Foxy Loxy.

"We are off to tell the king that the sky is falling in," clucked Chicken Licken importantly.

"What a good thing I met you all," said Foxy Loxy with a cunning smile. "I know the way, follow me."

So Chicken Licken, Henny Penny, Cocky Locky, Ducky Lucky, Drakey Lakey, Goosey Loosey and Turkey Lurkey all set off behind Foxy Loxy. He led them all straight to his den where he ate every single one of them for his dinner! So the king never heard that the sky was falling in. (It didn't, of course.)

The Three Little Pigs

an English folk tale

There once was a mother pig who had three little pigs. They were very poor indeed, and the day came when the mother pig could no longer look after the family. She sent the three little pigs out into the wide world to seek their fortunes.

The first little pig met a man carrying a big bundle of straw.

"Oh, please may I have that bundle of straw to build myself a house?" asked the first little pig. The man was tired of carrying the bundle of straw so he gladly gave it to the first little pig.

The first little pig built a very fine house out of the bundle of straw, and he lived there very happily. Then along came a big bad wolf.

"Little pig, little pig, let me come in!" shouted the wolf.

"No, no, not by the hair on my chinny chin chin. I'll not let you in," squeaked the first little pig.

"Then I'll huff and I'll puff, and I'll blow your house down," yelled the wolf. And he did. He huffed and he puffed and he blew the straw house down. The first little pig ran away as fast as his trotters would carry him.

Now the second little pig met a man carrying a bundle of sticks.

"Oh, please may I have that bundle of sticks to build myself a house?" asked the second little pig. The man was tired of carrying the bundle of sticks so he gladly gave it to the second little pig.

The second little pig built a very fine house out of the bundle of sticks, and he lived there very happily. Then along came the big bad wolf.

"Little pig, little pig, let me come in!" shouted the wolf.

"No, no, not by the hair on my chinny chin chin. I'll not let you in," squeaked the second little pig.

"Then I'll huff and I'll puff, and I'll blow your house down," yelled the wolf. And he did. He huffed and he puffed and he blew the stick house down. The second little pig ran away as fast as his trotters would carry him.

Now the third little pig met a man carrying a big load of bricks.

"Oh, please may I have that load of bricks to build myself a house?" asked the third little pig. The man was very tired indeed from carrying the big load of bricks so he gladly gave it to the third little pig.

The third little pig built a very fine house out of the big load of bricks, and he lived there very happily. Then along came the big bad wolf.

"Little pig, little pig, let me come in!" shouted the wolf.

"No, no, not by the hair on my chinny chin chin. I'll not let you in," squeaked the third little pig.

"Then I'll huff and I'll puff, and I'll blow your house down," yelled the wolf. And he tried. He huffed and he puffed but he could not blow the brick house down.

"Little pig, little pig, I am coming down your chimney to get you," bellowed the wolf.

"Please yourself," called the third little pig who was busy with some preparations of his own.

"Little pig, little pig, I have my front paws down your chimney," threatened the wolf.

"Please yourself," called the third little pig who was still busy with some preparations of his own.

"Little pig, little pig, I have my great bushy tail down your chimney," called the wolf.

"Please yourself," called the third little pig who was now sitting in his rocking chair by the fireside.

"Little pig, little pig, here I come!" and with a great rush and a huge SPLOSH! the big bad wolf fell right into the big pot of boiling water that the clever little pig had placed on the fire, right under the chimney. The wolf scrabbled and splashed and scrambled out of the big pot and ran as fast as ever he could right

out of the front door. And he was never seen again. The third little pig managed to find his two brothers, and they went and fetched their mother. And they are all still living happily together in the little brick house.

Androcles and the Lion

a retelling from the Fables of Phaedrus

M any thousands of years ago there lived a poor slave called Androcles. Life was very miserable for slaves. They barely had enough to eat, and if they didn't work hard enough they were sent to Rome to be thrown to the lions.

One day, Androcles had a chance to escape. He didn't hesitate. He ran and ran, and ran again until he was utterly exhausted, so he crawled into a forest to hide until he regained his strength. He was just settling down to try to sleep when a great lion hobbled out from behind a tree. At first, Androcles was absolutely petrified. He was just

thinking how very unfair life
was that he should manage
to escape, only to be
eaten by a lion, when
he realised the lion was not about to jump on him, but was
holding out his paw helplessly. Androcles stepped cautiously
towards the lion. The paw was all swollen and bleeding,
and when Androcles looked closely he could see why.
There was a huge thorn stuck in between the claws, which
must have been causing the lion considerable pain.

Androcles pulled the thorn out, and cleaned the
wound before wrapping it in leaves to keep it dry. The
great lion licked Androcles with his very rough tongue and
then lay down beside him and went to sleep. He kept
Androcles warm all night. In the morning the lion slipped
away very early and Androcles continued on his way.

Years passed. But one day Androcles' luck ran out and

he was captured by his master's men and sent into the arena to fight. The trap door was opened and a huge lion came bounding up to Androcles. He closed his eyes, waiting for certain death. But then he felt a rough tongue licking his face. It was his lion! The crowds cheered with delight at this unexpected turn of events, and the emperor made Androcles tell the story of how he had taken the thorn out of the lion's paw. The emperor decided to free Androcles, and said that the lion could go with him. Androcles kept the lion's coat well brushed and his paws free of thorns, while the lion kept Androcles warm in bed at night, and so they both lived to a very ripe old age together.

The Ugly Duckling

a retelling from the original story by Hans Christian Andersen

The mother duck was waiting for her eggs to
hatch. Slowly the first shell cracked and first a
tiny bill and then a little yellow wing
appeared. Then with a great rush, a bedraggled yellow
duckling fell out. He stretched his wings and began to
clean his feathers. Soon he stood proudly beside his mother,
watching as his sisters and brothers all pushed their way
out of their shells.

There was only one shell left. It was the largest, and
the mother duck wondered why it was taking so much
longer than the others. She wanted to take her babies

down to the river for their first swimming lesson. There was a sudden loud crack, and there lay quite the biggest and ugliest duckling she had ever seen. He wasn't even yellow. His feathers were dull brown and grey.

"Oh dear," said the mother duck.

She led the family down to the river, the ugly duckling trailing along behind the others. They all splashed into the water, and were soon swimming gracefully, all except the ugly duckling who looked large and ungainly even on the water.

"Oh dear," said the mother duck.

The whole family set off for the farmyard where they were greeted with hoots and moos and barks and snorts from all the other animals.

"Whatever is that?" said the rooster, pointing rudely at the ugly duckling. All the other ducklings huddled round their mother and tried to pretend the ugly duckling was not with them.

"Oh dear," said the mother duck.

The ugly duckling felt very sad and lonely. No one seemed to like him, so he ran away from the farmyard and hid in some dark reeds by the river. Some hunters came by with their loud noisy guns and big fierce

dogs. The ugly duckling paddled deeper into the reeds, trembling with fear. Only later in the day, as it was growing dark, did the ugly duckling dare move from his hiding place.

All summer he wandered over fields and down rivers. Everywhere he went people laughed and jeered at him, and all the other ducks he met just hissed at him or tried to bite his tail. As well as being ugly, the duckling was very lonely and unhappy. Soon winter came and the rivers began to freeze over. One day the duckling found himself trapped in the ice. He tucked his head under his wing, and decided that his short life must have come to an end.

He was still there early the next morning when a farmer came by on his way to feed the cows in the fields. The farmer broke the ice with his shoe, and wrapped the ugly duckling in his jacket then carried him home to his children. They put the poor frozen ugly duckling in a box by the fire, and as he thawed out they fed him and stroked his feathers. And there the ugly duckling stayed through the winter, growing bigger all the time.

Now the farmer's wife had never had much time for the ugly duckling. He was always getting under her feet in the kitchen, and he was so clumsy that he kept knocking things over. He spilt the milk in the bucket from the cow. He put his great feet in the freshly churned butter. He was just a nuisance, and one day the farmer's wife had enough. So, in a rage, she chased him out of her kitchen, out of the farmyard and through the gate down the lane.

It was a perfect spring day. The apple trees were covered in blossom, the grass was green and the air was filled with the sound of birdsong. The ugly duckling wandered down to the river, and there he saw three magnificent pure white swans. They were beautiful and so graceful as they glided over towards the bank where he

stood. He waited for them to hiss at him and beat the
water with their great wings to frighten him away, but
they didn't do any such thing. Instead they called him to
come and join them. At first he thought it was a joke, but
they asked him again.

He bent down to get into the
water, and there looking back
at him was his own reflection.
But where was the ugly
duckling? All he could see was
another great and magnificent
swan. He was a swan! Not an
ugly duckling but a swan. He
lifted his great long elegant neck,
and called in sheer delight, "I am a
swan! I am a SWAN!"and he sailed
gracefully over the water to join his real family.

The Three Billy Goats Gruff

a folk tale from Europe

In a mountain valley beside a rushing river, there lived three billy goats. One was very small, one was middle-sized and one was huge, and they were called the Three Billy Goats Gruff. Every day they would eat the lush green grass beside the river, and they were very content.

One day, however, the Three Billy Goats Gruff decided they would like to cross the river and see if the grass was any greener on the other side. The grass was actually no greener, nor was it any tastier, but they all felt they would like a change. First they had to find a way to cross the rushing river. They trotted a good way upstream before they found a little wooden bridge. After a good supper of lush green grass, they decided to wait until the next morning before crossing the little wooden bridge, so they settled down for the night.

Now, what the Three Billy Goats Gruff did not know was that under the little wooden bridge there lived a very mean and grumpy troll. He could smell the Three Billy Goats Gruff, and he thought they smelled very good to eat. So the next morning when the Three Billy Goats Gruff had had a good breakfast of lush green grass, the troll was hiding under the little wooden bridge, waiting for his chance to have a good breakfast too.

"That little wooden bridge does not look too strong,"

said the very small Billy Goat Gruff. "I will go across first to see if it is safe," and he trotted across the little wooden bridge. But when he was only halfway across, the mean and grumpy troll leapt out of his hiding place.

"Who is that trit-trotting across my bridge?" he roared. "I am going to eat you up!"

But the very small Billy Goat Gruff wasn't ready to be eaten up just yet, so he bravely said to the mean and grumpy troll, "You don't want to eat a skinny, bony thing like me. Just wait till my brother comes across, he is much bigger," and with a skip and a hop, the very small Billy Goat Gruff ran across the bridge to the lush green grass on the other side.

The middle-sized Billy Goat Gruff started to cross the

little wooden bridge, but when he was only halfway across, the mean and grumpy troll roared at him.

"Who is that trit-trotting across my bridge?" he roared. "I am going to eat you up!"

But the middle-sized Billy Goat Gruff wasn't ready to be eaten up just yet either, so he bravely said to the mean and grumpy troll,

"You don't want to eat a skinny, bony thing like me. Just wait till my brother comes across, he is even bigger," and with a skip and a hop, the middle-sized Billy Goat Gruff ran across the bridge to the lush green grass on the other side.

Now the huge Billy Goat Gruff had been watching all the time. He smiled to himself and stepped out onto the little wooden bridge. By this time the mean and grumpy troll was getting very hungry indeed, and he was even meaner and grumpier when he was hungry. He didn't even bother to hide, but stood in the middle of the bridge looking at the huge Billy Goat Gruff who came trotting up to him.

"Who is that trit-trotting across my bridge?" he roared. "I am going to eat you up!"

"Oh no, you won't!" said the huge Billy Goat Gruff, and he lowered his head and with his huge horns he biffed the mean and grumpy troll into the rushing river. The water carried him far away down the river, and he was never seen again. The Three Billy Goats Gruff lived happily for many more years eating the lush green grass, and they were able to cross the river just whenever they wanted!

The Greedy Dog

an English tale

There was once a very greedy dog who just ate and ate. Whenever he saw anything that looked good enough to eat, he would just open his mouth and gobble it all up. The postman wouldn't come near the house anymore, ever since the greedy dog mistook his ankle for an early breakfast. He would stand at the gate and throw the letters in the general direction of the letterbox. The paperboy just refused to go anywhere near. Visitors knew they had to come with a juicy bone or they wouldn't get as far as the front door.

One day the greedy dog was out wandering round

the shops. He loved doing this as there were always lots of really good smells for him to investigate, and sometimes old ladies, who didn't know any better, would give him sticky buns to eat.

As he walked past the butcher's shop, the greedy dog started to lick his lips. There in the window was a great big steak. It looked juicy and very good to eat. The greedy dog decided that the steak would make a very nice meal. So he watched and waited outside the shop. Soon one of his favourite old ladies walked down the street and into the butcher's shop. The greedy dog sidled in alongside the unsuspecting old lady. She wanted sausages and mince and goodness knows what else, so while the butcher was looking after her, the greedy dog pounced. He grabbed the steak and galloped out of the shop before anyone really had time to realise what was happening.

Then there was a great hue and cry. The butcher ran out of his shop with a bellow of rage, the little old lady fainted, and everyone in the street joined in the chase. But the greedy dog knew all the back streets, and he was soon far away and longing to eat his steak. He ran through the back streets until he came to the canal. He was just about to cross the bridge when he caught sight of another dog, right in front of him, and this dog also had a great juicy steak in his mouth! Well now, you and I know that what he was looking at was his own reflection, but the greedy dog did not know that. All he saw was a second steak that he might have so, with a great fierce bark, he leapt at the other dog.

But instead of gaining another meal, the greedy dog found himself very wet indeed, and he had lost his own steak! It would be good if I could tell you that from that day onwards the greedy dog was better behaved. But I am afraid his manners did not improve, and he is still looking for the other dog . . .

The Cat and the Mouse

a retelling from the original story by the Brothers Grimm

Now this is the tale of a wily cat and a foolish mouse. The mouse lived in a bare mouse hole under the pulpit in the church. The cat lived on an old cushion in the vestry. They had met on several occasions, the mouse usually whisking herself away very fast to the safety of her hole. She did not like the look of the cat's claws.

But one day, the cat called on the mouse at home.

"Miss mouse," a purry voice said, "why don't you and I set up home together? We could live in the bell tower and look after each other. We could share our food, too."

The mouse thought about this carefully. She had never been fond of cats ever since her great grandfather had been supper for the farm tom cat one cold frosty night. But she could see that there would be benefits. The cat had a nice smile on his face. So she agreed.

They put their savings together and bought a pot full of fat for the winter. The cat said he would hide it away safely under the altar where no one ever went, and so it was done. They both promised not to touch it until the weather became really bad.

The mouse went about her business, quite happy in her new home, although she found the stairs a wearisome business. But the cat could not stop thinking about the pot of fat. So he thought up a plan.

"Miss mouse, my cousin has just had a kitten," he said looking at the mouse. "And she wants me to be godcat. I should like to go to the christening, would you mind?"

"Not at all, Mister cat," said the mouse. "I have plenty to do today."

But the wicked Cat went straight to the pot of fat and ate the top off. Then he went to sleep for the rest of the day. When it was evening, he stretched and strolled back up to the bell tower.

"Did you have a nice time?" asked the mouse

"Oh yes, very nice," said the not very nice cat.

"And what is the kitten called?"

"Topoff," replied the cat.

"Topoff?" asked the mouse. "That is a very strange name. Still I suppose cats have different family names," and she went on with her work.

All went quietly for a few days but then the cat had great longings for the pot of fat again so he went to the mouse.

"I find I have another new godkitten. Would you mind if I went to the christening?" said the cat, his green eyes half closed.

"Another godkitten?" said the mouse. "My, my you do have a big family."

And the beastly cat slunk off and ate up half the pot of fat. When he sauntered back up the stairs that night the mouse was waiting.

"Well, how did it all go?" she said. "What is this kitten to be called?"

"Halfempty," replied the cat.

"Halfempty?" said the mouse. "I have never heard such a thing before."

But the cat was asleep, a secret smile twitching his whiskers.

Well, as you can imagine, it was not long before that greedy cat wanted some fat again.

"Miss mouse, just imagine! I have yet another godkitten. I should really go to this christening too," said the cat.

Miss mouse thought it all very strange but she was a kindly creature so she waved the cat off to yet another

christening. The cat, of course, just scuttled downstairs, slid under the altar and licked the pot of fat quite clean. He came back very late that night.

"Now what strange name did your family give this new kitten?" asked the mouse crossly. She had a headache from all the noise in the tower when the bells rang.

"Allgone," said the cat.

"Topoff, Halfempty and now Allgone!" the Mouse said in disbelief. "Well, I am very glad I am not a member of your family. I couldn't be doing with such weird names," and she went to sleep with her paws over her ears.

There were no more christenings for a while. The weather became colder and colder, and the mouse began to think of the little pot of fat hidden under the altar.

"Mister cat," she said one frosty morning, "I think it is time we collected our pot of fat. I am looking forward to a lick."

We will see about that thought the cat, but he padded downstairs behind the mouse. She reached under the altar and brought out the pot, but of course when she looked in it was all empty.

"What a foolish mouse I have been!" she cried. "Now I see what a wicked cat you have been. Topoff, Halfempty and Allgone indeed!"

"Such is the way of cats," said the greedy cat, and he put out a paw to grab mouse. But she was too quick for him, and dived back into her dear little mouse hole under the pulpit.

Never again did she trust cats, ever, ever.

PUSS IN BOOTS

retold from the original tale by Charles Perrault

A certain miller was so poor that when he died, all he left his three sons were his mill, his mule and a cat.

"Bagsy me the mill," said the eldest son.

"Bagsy me the mule," said the middle son.

"Oh, great!" said the youngest son. "I suppose I'm left with the cat then." (As you can tell, he wasn't very happy about it. But youngest children often start off with a bad deal in fairytales, so he should really have seen it coming.)

"Stop your moaning!" scolded the cat. "If you stick

with me, I can guarantee that you'll be thanking your dear old dad later. Now fetch me a large bag and leave me to get on with things. Oh – and get me a smart pair of boots made from the finest red leather, just like I've always wanted . . ."

The youngest son didn't argue. Firstly, the cat had never talked before, so he was speechless with shock. And secondly, he didn't have a better plan to suggest anyway. So he took what little money he had saved under the mattress and did exactly what the cat had told him . . .

As soon as Puss had finished purring with delight at how fine he looked in his smart boots of the finest red leather, he hurried along to a field and lay down quite still with his bag wide open beside him. After a while – hop! hop! hop! – along came a plump bunny. Pop! the silly rabbit jumped straight into the bag. Zip! Puss shut the bag. Whistling merrily, he took his catch to the palace and

presented it to the king. "My master, the
Marquis of Carabas, sends you this
gift," Puss announced, bowing low.

"Give him my warmest
thanks," the king announced,
smiling graciously.

As soon as Puss was
gone, the king turned to
his chamberlain and
whispered: "Whoever this Marquis is, he
must be very rich and important to send his messengers in
such smart boots!"

The next day the cat was back again – with a
present of two partridges. And the day after that – with
three pheasants. Every day for three months, Puss arrived
at court with a gift for the king from his master, the
Marquis of Carabas. "What a thoughtful, kind-hearted

man this Marquis of Carabas is!" the king exclaimed as his royal pantry filled up with delicious game.

One day, Puss learned that the king was going to take a drive along the river with his beautiful daughter. "Right, you're going for a swim!" the cat commanded the miller's youngest son.

"But – but – I don't have any swimming trunks!" the Marquis of Carabas protested, but Puss was already dragging him along to a certain spot on the riverbank. Before he knew it, the cat had taken away all his clothes and he was swimming around obediently among the waterweed.

Just then, the royal carriage came trundling by. "Help! Help!" shouted Puss, running out onto the road and flagging it down. "The Marquis of Carabas is drowning!"

The princess squealed with fright as she peered out

of the carriage and saw a man splashing about in the water. At once, the king ordered his guards into the river to pull him out.

"Your majesty," purred the cat, as the soldiers began trying to give the startled miller's son the kiss of life. "As if it wasn't bad enough that the Marquis of Carabas has nearly drowned, while he was in the water, robbers have stolen all his clothes!"

The king tut-tutted and sent his chamberlain galloping back to the palace to bring a selection of his very own robes for the Marquis to wear.

Soon the miller's son was looking exceedingly handsome in the king's best suit, and the princess was blushing a deep pink. "It's the very least I can do in return for all the kind gifts you have been sending me!" the king said earnestly. The miller's son had no idea what the king was talking about, but he thought it best just to nod and smile all the same. "You will come and ride with us a while, won't you?" insisted the king, and the miller's son was ushered up into the royal carriage to sit next to the princess.

Puss was highly excited that his scheme was working, and he ran ahead down the road. By and by, he came to a hayfield of mowers, and he said, "Good people, if you don't tell the king that this field belongs to the Marquis of Carabas, I'll make you all into cat food."

It wasn't long before the royal carriage passed by and, sure enough, the king leaned out of the window and asked, "Who does this land belong to?"

"It b-b-b-belongs to the M-m-m-arquis of C-c-c-arabas," the terrified mowers stuttered.

"You have a fine estate," the king beamed at the

miller's youngest son, and the so-called Marquis nodded and smiled.

Soon the royal carriage came to a cornfield of harvesters. The miller's youngest son was just as surprised as the king to learn from the harvesters that the cornfield belonged to him, too! A little further down the road, and a group of dairymaids insisted that their cows belonged to the Marquis of Carabas.

"My!" the king grinned. "What splendid lands you have!" And the princess's cheeks turned rosy with pleasure.

While the royal carriage rolled along, Puss was a long way down the road at a fearful ogre's castle. It was the ogre who owned all the land that Puss had been giving to the Marquis of Carabas (though luckily, the ogre didn't know about that!). "Mr Ogre," began Puss politely. "I have come to pay my respects to you because I have heard that you have remarkable powers. Is it true that you can turn yourself from a big, hulking ogre into a tiny, sneaky mouse?"

"Easy-peasy!" growled the ogre. He disappeared before Puss's very eyes and suddenly there was a mouse scurrying about on the floor. It took Puss only a few seconds to pounce and gobble him up, and that was the end of the ogre.

By the time the royal carriage pulled up outside the castle, Puss was waiting outside to greet it. "Welcome to the home of the Marquis of Carabas," Puss announced proudly. The cat ushered the highly surprised miller's youngest son and his stunned royal guests inside, where they found a delicious banquet the servants had prepared for them at Puss's instructions.

"My dear Marquis," beamed the king. "I am most impressed with your riches – er, I mean generosity. If there's anything I can do for you, just say the word."

The miller's son glanced at the princess, who hissed under her breath, "Go on! Ask him!"

So the Marquis of Carabas cleared his throat and said, "Actually, I'd quite like to marry your daughter!" and the king roared with happy laughter.

The couple were married that very day, and the miller's youngest son lived as the rich and prosperous Marquis of Carabas for the rest of his life. So his story has a happy ending after all. (And that's what happens in fairytales, so he should really have seen it coming.) As for Puss – well, he lived happily at the castle too. There were plenty of mice to catch, and that's all he needed to be content – as well as his smart boots of the finest red leather, of course!

The Wonderful Tar Baby

retold from the original tale by Uncle Remus

Brer Fox was doing what he usually did – trying to catch Brer Rabbit. But he'd be danged if this time he didn't catch that pesky varmint once and for all! Brer Fox mixed up a big pot of sticky tar and pulled and patted it into the shape of a baby. Then he lolloped up the road, set the tar baby sitting in the dust, and went to lay low in the ditch.

By and by, Brer Rabbit came bouncing down the road. "Good morning," he greeted the tar baby, "nice day, ain't it?"

But the tar baby didn't utter a word.

"I SAYS," shouted Brer Rabbit, just in case the tar baby hadn't cleaned his ears recently,

"GOOD MORNING! NICE DAY, AIN'T IT?"

The tar baby just stared straight ahead.

"Ain't you got no manners?" Brer Rabbit asked, crossly.

Still the tar baby stayed silent.

By this time, Brer Rabbit was hopping from foot to foot, madder than a snake in a wasps' nest. "You'd better speak to me civil-like or else!" he hollered.

But the tar baby simply ignored Brer Rabbit.

"Well I guess you've done gone and asked for this!" Brer Rabbit shrieked. BLIP! he thumped the tar baby straight in the mouth – and his fist was stuck fast to the tar baby's face. "You let me go!" Brer Rabbit yelled. "Let me go – or I'll let you have another!" BLAM! Brer Rabbit socked the tar baby again and his other fist was glued tight to the tar baby's head. "I've warned you!" bellowed Brer

Rabbit. SMACK! he kicked the tar baby and was left hopping around on one leg. "Don't make me do this!" Brer Rabbit shouted. WALLOP! another kick and the tar baby was holding him off the ground. "Right, you've really had it now!" Brer Rabbit screamed. THUNK! he head-butted the tar baby and found himself stuck eye-to-eye with the cheeky critter.

All this time, Brer Fox had been holding on to so much laughter he thought he was going to burst. Now he leapt out of his hiding place and howled, "My, oh my, Brer Rabbit! What type of mess have you got yourself into this time?"

"I suppose you're gonna have yourself a tasty barbecued bunny for supper this evening," Brer Rabbit admitted.

"Yep! You said it," grinned Brer Fox, licking his lips.

"Well I'm glad you're going to dress me up with some sauce and warm me over your fire," Brer Rabbit smiled. "I'd much rather you did that than throw me in that briar patch over there."

Hang on a minute, thought Brer Fox, and his face fell. That no-good rabbit seems quite pleased about being roasted! "I've changed my mind," Brer Fox said out loud. "I'm gonna hang you instead."

"Ain't I glad it's good ol' hangin' and not being thrown in the briar patch!" sighed Brer Rabbit.

Brer Fox frowned. "I mean, I'm going to drown you!" he snarled.

"Fine, fine . . ." smiled Brer Rabbit gaily. "Dip me in the water and at least I'll die clean. Just don't throw me in that there briar patch, that's all!"

At that, Brer Fox was sure that the very worst thing

he could do to Brer Rabbit was to hurl him into the briar patch. He grabbed him round the waist and pulled him hard and – SHLUP! – Brer Rabbit came unstuck from the tar baby. Brer Fox spun round and round and round and – WHEEEEEEEE! – Brer Rabbit went sailing high into the air and came down – DONK! – into the briar patch.

Brer Fox began to smile contentedly. "I've bested that bunny once and for all!" he chuckled.

A high-pitched giggle came from the far side of the briar patch, and when Brer Fox squinted into the sunshine, he could just see Brer Rabbit hopping away into the distance. "I was born and bred in a briar patch, Brer Fox!" he was singing. "Hee hee! Born and bred in a briar patch!"

Brer Fox boiled with rage and thumped the very first thing that came to hand. And you know what that was, don't you?

The Hare and the Tortoise

retold from the original fable by Aesop

The day that Tortoise challenged Hare to a race, all the animals laughed so hard that their tummies ached. But Tortoise was fed-up with Hare whizzing round him all the time, teasing him about how slow he was. I'll show that Hare, if it's the last thing I do! Tortoise promised himself.

Hare thought that Tortoise's little joke was extremely funny. For that's all Hare thought it was – a joke. Hare never expected that Tortoise would actually go through with his mad idea. So his eyes nearly popped out of his head when he arrived at the starting line to see Tortoise already there, limbering up in a very slow, stiff, creaky sort of way.

"Be careful there, old chap!" Hare worried, as he realised his friend was serious. "You don't want to do yourself an injury."

"Don't worry about me," replied Tortoise. "You should be working out how you're going to beat me. Ha! You won't see me for dust!"

A huge crowd of animals had gathered to watch the race and they all cheered and clapped and jumped up and down at Tortoise's bold remark.

Suddenly, Hare started to feel rather annoyed. "All right then. If that's the way you want it!" he snapped. "I was going to give you a headstart, but obviously you won't be wanting one."

"No need," breezed Tortoise, although his little heart was pumping inside his shell. "First one to the windmill's the winner."

Hare peered into the distance. The windmill was three fields away. He could get there in under a minute without even losing his breath. But surely it would take Tortoise all day to reach it!

"Three! Twit-Two! One!" cried Barn-Owl, and Tortoise lifted one leg over the starting line amid thunderous applause.

The stunned Hare watched in amazement as Tortoise began to crawl slowly away. Well, you have to hand it to Tortoise! Hare thought, seeing the funny side of things again. He's certainly got a good sense of humour and a lot of guts!

Hare sat down next to the starting line under a shady tree. It was a beautiful sunny day and it was very pleasant to sit there in the dappled light, watching Tortoise amble peacefully into the field. Hare's eyes shut and his head drooped before he even realised he was sleepy . . .

Meanwhile, Tortoise was remembering what his dear old mum had told him as a child: Slow and steady does it, son. Slow and steady does it. And Tortoise kept on going and didn't give up . . .

Hare didn't wake up until the night air was so cold that it was freezing his whiskers. Where am I? he thought. And then suddenly he remembered the race. Hare leapt to his feet and squinted into the moonlight, but there was no sign of Tortoise. All at once, he heard a faint sound of cheering coming from a long way off, and he saw tiny dark figures jumping up and down around the windmill. "Surely not!" Hare gasped, and shot off over the fields like an arrow. He arrived at the windmill just in time to see all

the animals hoisting Tortoise – the champion! – on their shoulders. And of course, after that, Hare never ever teased his friend about being slow again.

Boys and Girls

The Sorcerer's Apprentice

a German folk tale

The sorcerer lived in a dusty room at the top of a very tall gloomy tower. His table was covered with bottles and jars full of strange-coloured potions, and bubbling mixtures filled the air with horrible smells. The walls of the tower were lined with huge old books. These were the sorcerer's spell books and he would let no one else look inside them.

The sorcerer had a young apprentice called Harry. He was a good but lazy boy who longed only to be able to do magic himself. The sorcerer had promised to teach him all he knew, but only when he thought Harry was ready.

One day the sorcerer had to visit a friend who was a warlock. The sorcerer had never left Harry alone in the tower before and he did not entirely trust him. Looking very fierce, the sorcerer gave Harry his instructions.

"I have a very important spell to conjure up tonight when I return, so I need the cauldron full of water from the well," he said. "When you have filled the cauldron, you can sweep the floor and then you must light the fire."

Harry was not best pleased. It would take many, many trips to the well to fill the cauldron, and he would have all those steps to climb each time. Perhaps the sorcerer could read his mind, for the last thing he said as he climbed out of the window to fly away on his small green dragon was, "Touch nothing!" and off he flew in a cloud of smoke and flame from the dragon.

Harry watched until the sorcerer was safely far out of sight, and then did precisely what he had been told not to. He took one of the old dusty spell books. For a while it was quiet in the tower, and then Harry found what he was looking for. It was a spell to make a broomstick obey orders. Harry didn't hesitate. He forgot the sorcerer's instructions and that magic can be very dangerous. He took the spell book and read out the spell in a quavery voice for, truth to tell, he was very nervous. Nothing happened. Harry tried again, and this time his voice was stronger.

The broomstick quivered and then stood up. It grabbed a bucket and jumped off down the stairs. Soon it was back, the bucket brimful of water which it tipped into the cauldron. Harry was delighted and smiled as the broomstick set off down the stairs again. Up and down the broomstick went and soon the cauldron was full.

"Stop, stop!" shouted Harry, but the broomstick just carried on, and on. Soon the floor was awash and then the bottles and jars were floating around the room. Nothing Harry could say would stop the broomstick, and so in desperation, he grabbed the axe that lay by the fireside and chopped the broomstick into pieces. To his horror, all the pieces of wood turned into new broomsticks and they set off downstairs to the well, buckets appearing magically in their hands.

By now the water was nearly up to the ceiling. Wet spell books spun round and round the room, and Harry

gave himself up for lost.
Suddenly there was a
great clatter of wings and
a hiss of steam as the green
dragon flew into the tower. The
sorcerer was back! In a huge voice he
commanded the broomsticks to stop. They did. Then he
ordered the water back into the well. It all rushed back
down the stairs. Then he ordered the dragon to dry
everything with its hot breath. Then he turned to look at
Harry. And, oh dear! Harry could see that the sorcerer was
very, very angry indeed. The sorcerer looked as if he might
turn Harry into something terrible, but then he sat down
on a soggy cushion with a squelch.

"Right, I think it is time I taught you how to do
magic PROPERLY!" And he did.

Goldilocks and the Three Bears

a retelling from the original tale by Andrew Lang

Once upon a time there was a little girl called Goldilocks who lived in the middle of a great forest with her mother and her father. Now ever since she was tiny, her mother had told her she must never, ever wander off into the forest for it was full of wild creatures, especially bears. But as Goldilocks grew older she longed to explore the forest.

One washday, when her mother was busy in the kitchen, hidden in clouds of steam, Goldilocks sneaked off down the path that led deep into the forest. At first she was happy, looking at the wild flowers and listening to the birds singing, but it did not take long for her to become hopelessly lost.

She wandered for hours and hours and, as it grew darker, she became frightened. She started to cry, but then she saw a light shining through the trees. She rushed forward, sure she had somehow found her way home, only to realise that it was not her own cottage that she was looking at. But she opened the door and looked inside.

On a scrubbed wooden table there were three bowls of steaming hot porridge; a big one, a middle-sized one and a little one. Goldilocks was so tired that she quite forgot all her manners and just sat down at the table. The big bowl was too tall for her to reach. The middle-sized bowl was too hot. But the little one was just right, so she ate all the porridge up.

By the warm fire there were three chairs: a big one, a middle-sized one and a little one. Goldilocks couldn't climb up into the big one. The middle-sized one was too hard. The little was just the right size, but as soon as she sat down, it broke into pieces. Goldilocks scrambled to her feet and then noticed there were steps going upstairs, where she found three beds: a big one, a middle- 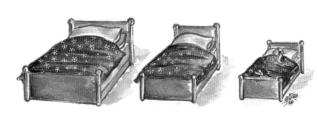 sized one and a little one. The big bed was too hard. The middle-sized one was too soft. But the little one was just right and she was soon fast asleep.

The cottage belonged to three bears, and it was not long before they came home. They knew at once that someone had been inside.

Father Bear growled, "Who has been eating my porridge?"

Mother Bear grumbled, "Who has been eating my porridge?"

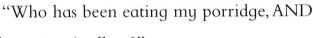

And Baby Bear gasped, "Who has been eating my porridge, AND has eaten it all up?"

The bears looked round the room. They looked at the chairs by the warm fire.

Father Bear growled, "Who has been sitting in my chair?"

Mother Bear grumbled, "Who has been sitting in my chair?"

And Baby Bear gasped, "Who has been sitting in my chair, AND has broken it to bits?"

The bears all clumped upstairs. They looked at the three beds.

Father Bear growled, "Who has been sleeping in my bed?"

Mother Bear grumbled, "Who has been sleeping in my bed?"

And Baby Bear gasped, "Who has been sleeping in my bed, AND is still there?"

Suddenly Goldilocks woke up. All she could see was three very cross-looking bears. She jumped off the bed, ran down the stairs, and out of the door. She ran and ran and ran, and by good fortune found herself outside her own cottage. Her mother and father scolded, but then gave her lots of hugs and kisses, and a big bowl of soup. Goldilocks had certainly learnt her lesson, and she never ever wandered off again.

Peter and the Wolf

original libretto by Sergey Prokofiev

P eter lived with his grandfather at the edge of the forest. Peter used to play with the wild birds and animals in the garden, but his grandfather always warned him not to go into the meadow in case the wolf crept out of the forest.

I am afraid Peter did not always do as he was told, so one day he slipped through the garden gate and into the meadow when he met a duck swimming in the middle of the pond.

"You must watch out for the wolf," said Peter to the duck but she was too busy enjoying herself to listen.

Round and round the pond she swam. A little bird flew down and the duck tried to persuade her to come into the pond as well. But as the little bird stood talking to the duck, Peter saw the cat sneak up behind her.

"Look out!" shouted Peter and the bird flew up to safety in the tree.

"Thank you, Peter," she said. The cat was not so pleased. Just then Peter's grandfather came out and saw the open garden gate.

"Peter! How many times do I have to tell you? Come back into the garden at once," he shouted and Peter walked slowly back in.

Meanwhile, at the far side of the meadow, nearest the forest, a grey shape slunk out from under the trees. It was the wolf!

The little bird flew up into the tree, and the cat joined her, although on a lower branch. But the duck was too

busy swimming to see what was happening and in a flash the wolf grabbed her and swallowed her whole!

Peter saw it all from the garden.

"I am going to catch that old wolf," he said to himself.

He found a piece of rope and climbed up a tree whose branches overhung the meadow. He made a loop in the rope and hung it out of the tree. Then he called to the little bird, "Can you tempt the wolf this way by flying round his head, please? I am going to catch him!"

The brave little bird darted down very close to the wolf's nose. The wolf snapped his fierce teeth, and only just missed the little bird. Closer and closer they came to the tree where Peter was hiding. The wolf was so busy trying to catch the bird that he did not see the rope. Peter looped it over the wolf's tail, and there he was, dangling from the branch of the tree!

Peter's grandfather came out and he was astonished to see the wolf. Then some hunters came out of the forest.

"Well done," they cried, "you have caught the wolf. We have been after him for a long time."

And they all went off in a very joyful procession to the zoo. Peter led the wolf at the front, the little bird flew overhead, and the cat padded alongside, taking care not to get too close to the wolf. The hunters came up in the rear with Peter's grandfather. And from deep inside the wolf's tummy, the duck quacked loudly, just to remind everyone that she was there!

Dick Whittington and his Cat

an English myth

Hundreds of years ago there lived a poor orphan boy called Dick Whittington. His only possession was his cat, but everyone in his village looked after him, so he never wanted for a meal or clothes on his back. In return, he worked hard wherever he was needed. Now Dick's greatest dream was to visit the great city of London where, he had heard, the streets were paved with gold.

One day, a waggoner pulled into the village to give his two great shire horses a drink. Dick offered to rub the horses down, and before long he was telling the waggoner

all about his great dream of visiting London town.

"Well, you must be in luck today," smiled the waggoner, "for that is where I am bound. Why don't you come with me and I will drop you off back here again when I return tomorrow?"

This was too good an offer to refuse, so Dick and his cat waved goodbye to the villagers and set off with the waggoner for London. When they arrived, Dick looked round about in astonishment. Never before had he seen such huge buildings, all crowded so closely together. And there were so many people! Dick set off to explore, promising the waggoner he would be back in the evening.

The pavements certainly did not appear to be made of gold. But he kept on thinking he should just try round the next corner, and then the next and, before long, Dick realised that he was hopelessly lost. He stumbled into a doorway, and worn out with hunger and worry at not keeping his promise to help the waggoner, he fell asleep.

Now as luck would have it, Dick had chosen a very good doorway to sleep in. The house belonged to a rich merchant, Mr Fitzwarren, who was very kind and always willing to help anyone in need. So when he came home later that evening, Mr Fitzwarren took Dick and his cat indoors and told the cook to give him supper. The cook was very grumpy indeed at having to prepare a meal late at night for Dick who, she thought, looked like a ragamuffin.

The next morning, Dick told Mr Fitzwarren the whole story. Smiling, Mr Fitzwarren told Dick that, as he had found, the streets of London were not paved with gold, and indeed life there was very hard.

"But you look like a strong boy, would you like to

work for me, Dick?" he asked. "You will have a roof over your head and a good dinner every day in return for helping in the kitchen and the stables."

Dick was delighted, and he soon settled into the household. He worked hard, and everyone liked him, except the cook. She gave him all the really horrible jobs in the kitchen and would never let him have a moment's rest. But she didn't dare defy her master and so Dick had his good dinner every day.

Now whenever one of Mr Fitzwarren's ships went to sea, it was his custom to ask everyone in the household to give something to the ship's cargo for luck. Poor Dick had only his cat and it was with a very heavy heart that he handed her over.

The ship was at sea for many, many months before they finally came to port in China. The captain and the crew went ashore to show the emperor the cargo they had

brought all the way from London. The
emperor had known the captain for
many years and they were old
friends, so they sat down to a state
banquet before discussing business.
But to the emperor's great
embarrassment, the entire meal was
ruined by the rats that boldly ran everywhere,
even over the plates they were eating off. The emperor
explained that they had tried everything but nothing could
rid the court of the plague of rats. The captain smiled.

"I think I have the answer," he said and he sent for
Dick's cat. Within moments of her arrival, there were piles
of dead rats at the emperor's feet. He was so impressed that
he gave the captain a ship full of gold just for the cat.

Back in London, Dick's life was a misery. The cook
was nastier than ever and he didn't even have his beloved

cat for company, so one day he ran away, intending to walk home to his village. But he had not gone far before he heard the church bells ringing, and they seemed to say,

"Turn again Dick Wittington,

Thrice Lord Mayor of London."

Dick didn't know what the bells meant, but he remembered how kind Mr Fitzwarren had been, so he turned round again and went back before the cook had even noticed that he was missing. Of course when the ships came home, Mr Fitzwarren gave Dick his fair share and more. This was the start of Dick's prosperity, and he even married Mr Fitzwarren's daughter, Jane. He did become Lord Mayor of London three times, but he never forgot his early days of poverty and he founded schools and hospitals for the poor. He and Jane had many children, and there were always lots of cats in their great house as well!

The Precious Stove

an Austrian folk tale

Peter lived with his mother and father and his brothers and sisters in an old wooden cottage deep in the woods of Austria. They were very poor and the cottage had hardly any furniture, and they might have been very cold in winter were it not for their most treasured possession, a stove. This was no ordinary stove. It was made of white porcelain and it was so tall the gold crown at the top almost scraped the ceiling. Its feet were carved like lion's claws, the talons painted gold. The sides of the stove were painted with flowers and rare birds, in glowing colours, and the door was tiled in blue and

gold. It looked very out of place in
the poor wooden cottage for it
had originally been made for a
king's palace. Many years before,
Peter's grandfather had rescued it,
after a great war, from the ruins of
the palace where he used to work.

Peter used to draw copies of the flowers and birds
on pieces of brown paper with a stub of old pencil.

One evening, as Peter and his sister Gilda lay curled
up in the warmth at the foot of the stove, their father
came in, shaking the snow from his boots. He looked tired
and ill.

"My children, this is the last night you will be able to
enjoy our beautiful stove," he said sadly. "Tomorrow it will
be taken away as I have had to sell it. We have no money
left, and we need food more than we need a grand stove."

The children were horrified, but their father would not change his mind. That night, instead of banking up the stove to keep it burning warmly through the night, he let the fire die down so it was quite cold in the morning. The traders arrived and loaded the stove onto a cart, and off it rumbled down the track towards the town. Peter's mother and father looked at the handful of gold coins the traders had given them and shook their heads. It seemed a poor bargain when all was said and done.

Peter and Gilda whispered together outside behind the wood pile.

"You have to follow the cart, Peter," said Gilda, "so you can see where our stove goes."

So Peter rushed off down the track after the cart, pausing only to stuff a couple of apples into his pocket. The journey into town was slow as the stove was heavy so the cart could not travel very fast, but by evening it had reached the station. Peter crept as close as he dared, and heard the traders arranging for the stove to go to Vienna by train the very next morning. He made up his mind very quickly. Once the traders had gone to an inn for the night, he clambered up and inside the stove. There was plenty of room inside for a small boy, and he knew that air would come in from the grill at the top under the golden crown. He soon fell fast asleep.

When he awoke, the train was moving fast. It sped through snowy forests and past the mighty Danube river. Peter munched his apples and wondered what his parents would be thinking, and just where was he going to end up, and then what could he do, anyway, to keep the stove for his family.

Eventually the train came to a halt and with much banging and clattering all the boxes around the stove were unloaded onto the platform. Then Peter heard a gruff voice.

"Have a care there! That valuable stove is going to the palace, take care it isn't damaged in any way or it will be the worse for you!"

The palace! Peter's knees shook. The palace, why that was where the king lived. Peter sat as quiet as a mouse as he felt the stove lifted up off the train and onto another cart. It clattered through cobbled streets and over a wooden bridge, and then came to a halt. Many voices came through the grill as the stove was moved off the cart.

"My word, the king will be pleased! Look what a fine stove it is," said one voice.

"It must have come from a palace originally, look at the golden crown at the top," said another.

Then there was silence for a while. Peter strained his ears, and his knees shook a little more. Then he heard the swishing of long robes on a polished floor, and a murmur of voices. Then a deep hush.

"Truly, it is a very beautiful stove. I did not expect it to be so fine. Look at the quality of the painting round the sides," said a deep important voice. And then the handle of the door turned and light flooded into the stove. Peter tumbled out onto the floor as the same deep voice said, "Good gracious! What have we here, a child in the stove!"

Peter picked himself up and looked up into eyes that were full of laughter. They belonged to a man dressed in a bright red jacket with great gold tassels and gold buttons. Many glittering medals gleamed on his chest. A great silver sword hung by his side. It was the king!

Peter was absolutely terrified, but the king kept on smiling.

"Well, my boy, would you like to tell me how you come to be inside my new stove?"

A servant rushed forward and grabbed Peter by the arm, meaning to drag him away, but the king raised his hand and the man stepped back.

"Let the child speak," said the king.

Well, once Peter found his tongue, he could not stop. He told the king all about the stove. How it had stood in their poor cottage for as long as he could remember. How much the family welcomed its heat in the winter. And he told the king that his father had been forced to sell the stove for a few gold pieces to buy food.

The king listened in silence while Peter told his story.

"Peter, I am not going to give you back your stove for it belongs here in the palace, but I will give your father several bags of gold, for it is a very valuable stove. And perhaps you would like to stay here and look after it for me?" he asked.

Peter was delighted. And he looked after the stove for the king from that day on. His family never wanted for food again, and every summer they would all come to stay at the palace to see Peter, and the stove of course. When the king discovered how good Peter was at drawing, he sent him to art school and he became a very fine artist. But when he was an old man, all his grandchildren wanted to hear was the story of how he came to Vienna inside a stove!

Little Red Riding Hood

a retelling from the original tale by Charles Perrault

There was once a little girl who lived in the middle of a deep dark forest with her mother and father, who was a woodcutter. The little girl always wore a red cloak with a warm hood and so she was called Little Red Riding Hood.

One day she decided to visit her granny who lived some way from the woodcutter's cottage. She took a basket with a cake her mother had baked and set off. Now the last thing her mother had said to Little Red Riding Hood was, "Don't leave the path, and don't talk to any strangers," but I am afraid Little Red Riding Hood was not really listening. So when she saw some bluebells growing under a tree she left the path and began to pick a bunch for her granny. Slowly, slowly she wandered further away from the path, deeper into the trees. Suddenly, she was not alone. There in front of her stood a great big wolf. Now Little Red Riding Hood had not met a wolf before so she did not realise that wolves are not the kind of people it is wise to be too friendly with.

"Good day, little girl," said the wolf with a snarly sort of a smile. "What is your name and where are you going?"

"My name is Little Red Riding Hood. I am going to visit my granny, and I am taking her a cake to eat," replied Little Red Riding Hood.

The wolf was delighted. Not only a little girl to eat but a granny AND a cake as well!

"And where does your granny live, little girl?" asked the wolf, trying hard to smile nicely despite his fierce teeth.

Little Red Riding Hood told the wolf where her granny lived, and went on picking bluebells. The wolf slipped away through the trees and soon found the granny's cottage. He tapped on the door and said, in a disguised voice, "Hello, granny. It is Little Red Riding Hood. I have brought you a cake, will you let me in?"

As soon as the door was open, the wolf bounded in, and gobbled the granny all up! He put on her nightcap and shawl and climbed into her bed. Soon he heard Little Red Riding Hood coming and he tried his snarly smile again.

"Hello, granny," said Little Red Riding Hood. "I have brought you a cake and these bluebells," and she came up to the bedside.

"Goodness, granny! What great big eyes you have!" she said.

"All the better to see you with," growled the wolf.

Little Red Riding Hood could not help noticing the wolf's teeth.

"Goodness, granny! What great big teeth you have!"

"All the better to eat you with!" snapped the wolf and gobbled Little Red Riding Hood up. He gobbled up the cake in the basket as well and then, very full indeed, he fell fast asleep, snoring loudly.

Now by great good luck, Little Red Riding Hood's father was passing by the cottage, and when he heard the terrible snores he put his head round the door to see who was making such a noise. He was horrified to see the wolf

so he took his axe and made a great slit down the wolf's tummy. Out jumped Little Red Riding Hood. Out staggered granny. She stitched up the wolf's tummy and told him to mind his manners in future. Then, as there was no cake left for tea, they all went back home, and Little Red Riding Hood's mother made pancakes. I am pleased to say Little Red Riding Hood had learnt her lesson, and she never spoke to wolves again.

The Gingerbread Boy

an English folk tale

One fine sunny day, an old woman was making some ginger biscuits. She had a little dough left over and so she made a gingerbread boy. She gave him raisins for eyes and cherries for buttons, and put a smile on his face with a piece of orange peel. And she popped him in the oven. But as she lifted the tray out of the oven when the biscuits were cooked, the gingerbread boy hopped off the tray and ran straight out of the door! The old woman ran after him, and her husband ran after her, but they couldn't catch the gingerbread boy. He called out, "Run, run, as fast as you

can! You can't catch me, I'm the gingerbread man!"

The old dog in his kennel ran after the old man and the old woman, but he couldn't catch the gingerbread boy. The ginger cat, who had been asleep in the sun, ran after the dog, but she couldn't catch the gingerbread boy. He called out,

"Run, run, as fast as you can! You can't catch me, I'm the gingerbread man!"

The brown cow in the meadow lumbered after the cat, but she couldn't catch the gingerbread boy. The black horse in the stable galloped after the cow but he couldn't catch the gingerbread boy. He called out,

"Run, run, as fast as you can! You can't catch me, I'm the gingerbread man!"

The fat pink pig in the sty trotted after the horse, but

she couldn't catch the gingerbread boy. The rooster flapped and squawked after the pig but he couldn't catch the gingerbread boy. He called out, "Run, run, as fast as you can! You can't catch me, I'm the gingerbread man!"

He ran and ran, and the old woman and the old man, the dog and the cat, the cow and the horse, the pig and the rooster all ran after him. He kept running until he came to the river. For the first time since he had hopped out of the oven, the gingerbread boy had to stop running.

"Help, help! How can I cross the river?" he cried.

A sly fox suddenly appeared by his side. "I could carry you across," said the sly fox.

The gingerbread boy jumped onto the fox's back, and the fox slid into the water.

"My feet are getting wet," complained the gingerbread boy.

"Well, jump onto my head," smiled the fox, showing a lot of very sharp teeth. And he kept on swimming.

"My feet are still getting wet," complained the gingerbread boy again after a while. "Well, jump onto my nose," smiled the fox, showing even more very sharp teeth.

The gingerbread boy jumped onto the fox's nose, and SNAP! the fox gobbled him all up. When the fox climbed out of the river on the other side, all that was left of the naughty gingerbread boy was a few crumbs. So the old woman and the old man, the dog and the cat, the cow and the horse, the pig and the rooster all went home and shared the ginger biscuits. They were delicious.

Jack and the Beanstalk

a retelling from the original tale by Joseph Jacobs

This is the story of how Jack did a silly thing, but all was well in the end.

Jack and his mother were very poor and there came a sad day when there was no more money left, so Jack was told to take the cow to market and sell her.

As Jack led the cow to market, he met a funny little man with a tall feather in his hat.

"And where might you be going with that fine-looking cow?" the funny little man asked.

Jack explained and the little man swept off his hat with the tall feather, and shook out five coloured beans.

"Well, young Jack, I can save you a journey. I will give you these five magic beans in exchange for your cow."

Now Jack should have realised that this was all rather odd, for how did the funny little man know his name? But once he heard the word "magic" he didn't stop to think. He took the beans at once, gave the funny little man the cow and ran off home to his mother.

"Jack, you are a complete fool! You have exchanged our fine cow for five worthless beans!" She flung the beans out of the window, and sent Jack to bed without any supper.

When he woke in the morning, Jack couldn't understand why it was so dark in the cottage. He rushed outside to find his mother staring in amazement at the most enormous beanstalk that reached right up into the clouds.

"I told you they were magic beans," smiled Jack, and without any hesitation he began to climb the beanstalk. He climbed and climbed until he could no longer see the ground below. When he reached the top there stood a vast castle. Jack knocked at the door, and it was opened by a HUGE woman!

"My husband eats little boys for breakfast so you better run away quickly," she said to Jack. But before Jack could reply, the ground started to shake and tremble.

"Too late!" said the giant's wife. "You must hide," and she bundled Jack into a cupboard. Jack peeped through the keyhole, and saw the most colossal man stump into the kitchen.

"Fee fi fo fum! I smell the blood of an Englishman!" he roared.

"Don't be silly, dear. You can smell the sausages I have just cooked for your breakfast," said the giant's wife, placing a plate piled high with one hundred and sixty-three sausages in front of him. The giant did not seem to have very good table manners, and had soon gobbled the lot. Then he poured a great bag of gold onto the table, and counted all the coins. With a smile on his big face, he soon fell asleep.

Jack darted out of the cupboard, grabbed the bag of money and hared out of the kitchen. He slithered down the beanstalk as fast as ever he could and there, still standing at the bottom, was his mother. She was astonished when she saw the gold.

Jack's mother bought two new cows and she and Jack were very content now they had plenty to eat. But after a while Jack decided he would like to climb the beanstalk again. The giant's wife was not very pleased to see him.

"My husband lost a bag of gold the last time you were here," she muttered looking closely at Jack, but then the ground began to shake and tremble. Jack hid in the cupboard again.

The giant stumped into the kitchen.

"Fee fi fo fum! I smell the blood of an Englishman!" he roared.

"Don't be silly, dear. You can smell the chickens I have just cooked for your breakfast," said the giant's wife, placing a plate piled high with thirty-eight chickens in front of him. The giant had soon gobbled the lot. Then he lifted a golden hen onto the table, and said, "Lay!" and the hen laid a golden egg. With a smile on his big face he fell asleep, snoring loudly.

Jack darted out of the cupboard, grabbed the golden hen and hared out of the kitchen. He slithered down the beanstalk as fast as ever he could and there, still standing at the bottom, was his mother. She was astonished when she saw the hen.

Jack's mother bought a whole herd of cows and found a farmer to look after them. She bought lots of new clothes for herself and Jack, and they were very content. But after a while Jack decided he would like to climb the beanstalk one last time. The giant's wife was not at all pleased to see him.

"My husband lost a golden hen the last time you were here," and she peered closely at Jack, but then the ground began to shake and tremble. This time Jack hid under the table.

The giant stumped into the kitchen.

"Fee fi fo fum! I smell the blood of an Englishman!" he roared.

"I would look in the cupboard if I were you," said the giant's wife, but of course the cupboard was empty. They were both puzzled. The giant trusted his nose, and his wife didn't know where Jack had gone.

"Eat your breakfast, dear. I have just cooked you ninety-two fried eggs," said the giant's wife, placing a plate in front of him. The giant had soon gobbled the lot. Then he lifted a golden harp onto the table, and said, "Play!" and the harp played so sweetly that the giant was soon fast asleep, snoring loudly.

Jack crept out from under the table and grabbed the golden harp, but as soon as he touched it the harp called

out, "Master, master!" and the giant awoke with a great
start. He chased after Jack who scrambled down the
beanstalk as fast as ever he could with the harp in his
arms. As soon as Jack reached the ground he raced to get a
big axe and chopped through the beanstalk. Down
tumbled the great beanstalk, down tumbled the giant and
that was the end of them both!

Jack and his mother lived very happily for the rest
of their days. The bag of gold never ran out, the hen laid
a golden egg every day, and the harp soon forgot
about the giant and played sweetly for
Jack and his mother.

Liam and the Fairy Cattle

an Irish legend

L iam and his mother lived by the sea. They had a small white cottage with a pile of peat for the fire outside, and a row of potatoes to eat with the fish that Liam would catch. They had two cows, and Liam's mother would make butter and cheese from their milk. She baked bread and gathered sweet heather honey from the hives at the bottom of the meadow. They did not have much in life, but they were happy.

But then there came a time when ill luck fell on the small white cottage. First the two cows died, one after the other, and there was no cheese to eat. Then the shoals of fish swam far out to sea and Liam would come home empty handed. The potatoes rotted in the ground, and Liam and his mother were hungry all the time.

One day when Liam was wandering along the shoreline he came across two boys throwing stones at a seal. He shouted at the boys and chased them away, but when he went to see if the seal needed help it turned its head once and looked deep into his eyes then slipped away into the sea. As it dived into the waves he saw blood on its head.

Three days later when Liam and his mother were sitting by the fire in the evening there came a knock at the door. There on the doorstep stood an old, old man leaning on a staff. His clothes looked wet through and he had a large cut on his forehead, but his eyes were gentle.

"I am very weary, might I come in and warm myself at your fire?" the old man asked.

Liam opened the door
wide, and bid the old
man come in. His
mother pulled up a
stool close to the
fire, and warmed
up the last of the
soup in the pot while
she bathed the wound
on his head. He thanked
her kindly, smiling at Liam,
and Liam had the strangest
feeling he had looked into those deep brown eyes before.
But he made up the fire for the night and they all slept
peacefully until the day.

The old man looked better for his night's shelter, and
as he rose to leave he spoke to Liam's mother.

"I have no money to offer you but I would like to thank you for your shelter and food, and I would like to repay the boy here for his kindness," and he turned and looked at Liam with his gentle brown eyes. "I know you have lost your cows so I will tell you where you can find some special cows who will give you milk such as you have never tasted before. Tonight is a full moon and the sea-folk will bring their cattle up out of the sea to graze on the lush green grass that grows just beyond the shoreline."

Liam's mother laughed.

"I have often heard tales of these marvellous cattle, but in all the years
I have lived here I have never
seen a fairy cow."

"That is because your eyes have not been opened by a touch with the heather that grows on the grave of Fionn who died all those years ago," said the old man and there in his hand he held out a sprig of heather. "Will you let me touch your eyes, and the boy's too? Then you shall see what you shall see."

Well, Liam's mother felt she had nothing to fear from this kindly old man and so both she and Liam let him touch their eyes with the sprig of heather.

"Now," he said, "you must gather seven handfuls of earth from the churchyard, and then tonight go to the

meadow just beyond the shoreline. There you will see the fairy cattle. Choose the seven you like the best and throw the earth onto each one. They will all run back to the sea, save the seven that you have chosen. Bring those seven back home and look after them in your kindly way and they will be with you always. Now I must return from whence I came. Liam, will you walk with me to the sea?" and the old man looked at Liam with those gentle eyes once again.

So Liam and the strange old man walked to the shoreline. One moment they were together on the sand, the next Liam was alone. But when he looked out to sea, there was a seal, looking at him with gentle brown eyes. Then with a ripple, it was gone under the waves.

That night, Liam and his mother did as the old man had bid. They gathered the earth from the churchyard and made their way quietly down to the meadow. There indeed was the herd of fairy cattle. They were small, no bigger than a sheepdog, and all colours, brown and black and white and brindled. Liam and his mother choose three black, three white and a brindled one, and Liam crept up behind them and threw the earth onto their backs. The rest of the herd scattered back down to the shore and ran into the waves where they quickly disappeared. But the seven in the meadow stood quietly and showed no fear as Liam and his mother led them home.

From that day on, Liam and his mother had a plentiful supply of rich creamy milk. The little fairy cattle would low gently in the byre and were well content with their life on land. But Liam would never let them out to graze when there was a full moon in case the sea-folk came to claim them back.

Royal Adventures

The Twelve Dancing Princesses

a retelling from the original story by the Brothers Grimm

The king was very puzzled. He had twelve daughters, each one as beautiful as the moon and the stars, and he loved them above all the riches in his kingdom. But every morning the princesses would appear yawning and bleary-eyed, and with their shoes worn quite through. Every evening the king would kiss them good night and lock the door behind him. So how did they get out? And where did they go? The princesses certainly were not letting on.

Buying new shoes every day was costing him a fortune so the king was determined to solve the mystery.

The court messenger was sent to all four corners of the kingdom to issue the king's proclamation that he would give the hand of one of his daughters in marriage to any man who could discover the secret. But should he fail after three nights he would be banished forever.

Needless to say there were plenty of young men willing to risk banishment to win such a prize. But they soon found the princesses were too clever by half. Before they retired for the night, the princesses sang and played their musical instruments and fed them sweetmeats and rich honeyed mead.

Before they realised it morning had come and there were the sleepy princesses and twelve pairs of worn-out shoes.

The king was beside himself. Only the court shoemaker went about with a smile on his face.

Now into the kingdom at this time there wandered a penniless soldier. He read the proclamation and had just decided to try his luck when an old woman came slowly down the dusty road. The young man offered her some of his

bread and cheese, and as they sat peaceably together the old woman asked where he was bound. When he had explained she said, "Well, I may be able to help you. You must not drink the mead those cunning princesses offer you, for it is drugged. Pretend to be asleep, and you shall see what you shall see. This may help you," and the old woman handed him a silvery cloak. "Whenever you wear this you will be invisible. Use it well!" and the old woman disappeared.

"Well, perhaps I will succeed now I have magic on my side," murmured the young man as he set off for the palace. By now the king was tearing his hair out. The court shoemaker had taken on extra cobblers to help keep up with the demand for new shoes every day. The princesses were falling asleep into their bowls of porridge at breakfast every morning.

The young man bowed deeply to the king and

smiled at all the princesses. He ate a hearty supper but when the eldest princess gave him a goblet of mead he only pretended to drink it. Then he yawned loudly and let his head droop as if he had fallen asleep.

The butler and the first footman dumped the young man onto the bed placed across the door of the princesses' bedchamber. He cautiously opened one eye and gazed around the room. The princesses were putting on gorgeous velvet and brocade dresses and rings and necklaces. They giggled and whispered as they brushed their hair, powdered their faces and then pulled on the brand new jewelled slippers that the shoemaker had only delivered a few hours earlier. The eldest princess clapped her hands three times. A trap door opened up in the floor and they all swiftly descended down a steeply curving staircase. Just as soon as the last princess had disappeared the young man flung the magic cloak round his shoulders and rushed after them.

He found himself in a wondrous garden where the trees were covered in rich jewels, sparkling in candlelight. Musicians played whirling tunes and he saw all the princesses dancing with the most handsome princes. The young man was spellbound, but he managed to keep his

wits about him. He reached up and broke off a branch from one of the jewelled trees and hid it under his cloak. Then he ran back and lay down on his bed as though he had never stirred. So it happened on the second and the third nights.

It was with a weary voice that the king asked the young man at breakfast on the fourth day if he had found out where the princesses went at night. The king sat up very quickly when the young man told his tale and produced the branches from the trees. The king was delighted and the young man chose the youngest sister for his bride. And they all lived happily ever after. Except, of course, the court shoemaker, who always made the young man's shoes just a little too tight so they pinched.

The Frog Prince

a retelling from the original story by the Brothers Grimm

Once upon a time, there lived a very spoilt princess who never seemed content. The more she had, the more she wanted. And she just would not do what she was told.

One day she took her golden ball out into the woods, although she had been told by her chief nanny that she must embroider some new handkerchiefs. She threw the golden ball high up into the sky once, twice, but the third time it slipped from her hands and, with a great splash, it fell down, down into a deep well. The princess stamped her foot and yelled, but this did not help. So she kicked the side of the well, and was just getting ready for another big yell, when a very large frog plopped out of the well.

"Ugh!" said the princess. "A horrible slimy frog, go away at once," but the frog didn't move. Instead, it spoke.

"What are you making such a fuss about?"

A talking frog! For a moment the princess was speechless, but then she looked down her nose and said,

"If you must know, my most precious golden ball has fallen down this well, and I want it back."

With a sudden leap, the frog disappeared down the well. In the wink of an eye, it was back with the golden ball. The princess went to snatch it up, but the frog put a wet foot rather firmly on it and said,

"Hasn't anyone taught you any manners? 'Please' and

'thank you' would not go amiss, and anyway I have a special request to make."

The princess looked at the frog in utter astonishment. No one ever dared talk to her like that, and certainly not a frog. She glared at the frog and said crossly,

"May I have my ball back, please, and what is your special request?"

The frog did not move its foot, but bent closer to the princess.

"I want to come and live with you in the palace and eat off your plate and sleep on your pillow, please."

The princess looked horrified, but she was sure a promise to a frog wouldn't count so she shrugged her shoulders and said, "Course you can," and grabbed her ball from frog and ran back to the palace very quickly.

That night at supper the royal family heard a strange voice calling,

"Princess, where are you?" and in hopped the frog.

"Oh bother!" said the princess. The queen fainted. The king frowned.

"Do you know this frog, princess?" he asked.

"Oh bother!" said the princess again, but she had to tell her father what had happened. When he heard the story, he insisted the princess keep her promise.

The frog ate very little, the princess even less. And when it was time to go to bed, the king just looked very sternly at the princess who was trying to sneak off on her own. She bent down and picked the frog up by one leg, and when she reached her great four-poster bed, she plonked the frog down in the farthest corner. She did not sleep a wink all night.

The next evening, the frog was back. Supper was a quiet affair. The queen stayed in her room, the king read the newspaper, and the princess tried not to look at the frog. Bedtime came, and once again the frog and the princess slept at opposite ends of the bed.

The third evening, the princess was terribly hungry so she just pretended the frog was not there and ate everything that was placed in front of her. When it came to bedtime, she was so exhausted that she fell in a deep sleep as soon as her head touched the pillow.

The next morning when she woke up, she felt much better for her good sleep until she remembered the frog. But it was nowhere to be seen. At the foot of the bed, however, there stood a very handsome young man in a green velvet suit.

"Hello, princess. Do you know that you snore?" he said.

The princess's mouth fell open ready to yell, but the handsome young man continued, "I don't suppose you recognise me, thank goodness, but I was the frog who rescued your golden ball. I was bewitched by a fairy who said I was rude and spoilt," and here the young man looked sideways at the princess whose mouth was still hanging open, "And the spell could only be broken by someone equally rude and spoilt having to be nice to me."

The princess closed her mouth. The king was most

impressed with the young man's good manners, and the queen liked the look of his fine green velvet suit. Everyone liked the fact that the princess had become a very much nicer person. Before long it seemed sensible for the princess and the handsome young man to get married. They had lots of children who were not at all spoilt and everyone lived happily ever after. The golden ball and the green velvet suit were put away in a very dark cupboard.

The Princess and the Pea

a retelling from the original story by Hans Christian Andersen

The prince was very fed up. Everyone in the court, from his father, the king, down to the smallest page, seemed to think it was time he was married. Now the prince would have been very happy to get married, but he did insist that his bride be a princess, a real true and proper princess. He had travelled the land and met plenty of nice girls who said they were princesses, but none, it seemed to him, were really true and proper princesses. Either their manners were not quite exquisite enough, or their feet were much too big. So he sat in the palace, reading dusty old history books and getting very glum.

One night, there was the most terrible storm. Rain was lashing down, and thunder and lightning rolled and flashed round the palace. The wind kept blowing out the candles, and everyone huddled closer to the fire. Suddenly there was a great peal from the huge front door bell.

And there, absolutely dripping wet, stood a princess. Well, she said she was a princess, but never did anyone look less like a princess. Her hair was plastered to her head, her dress was wringing wet and her silk shoes were covered in mud. She was quite alone, without even the smallest maid, and just where had she come from? But she kept insisting she was a princess.

We will see about that, thought the queen. While the dripping girl sat sipping a mug of warm milk and honey, the queen went to supervise the making of the bed in the second-best spare bedroom. She didn't think it necessary to put their late night visitor in the best spare bedroom, after all she might only be a common-or-garden duchess. The queen told the maids to take all the bedclothes and the mattress off the bed. Then she placed one single pea right on the middle of the bedstead. Next the maids piled twenty mattresses on top of the pea, and then twenty feather quilts on top of the mattresses. And thus the girl was left for the night.

In the morning, the queen swept into the bedroom in her dressing gown and asked the girl how she had slept.

"I didn't sleep a wink all night." said the girl. "There was a great, hard lump in the middle of the bed. It was quite dreadful. I am sure I am black and blue all over!"

Now everyone knew she really must be a princess, for only a real princess could be as soft-skinned as that. The prince was delighted, and insisted they got married at once, and they lived very happily ever after. They always slept in very soft beds, and the pea was placed in the museum, where it probably still is today.

The Emperor's New Clothes

retold from the original tale by Hans Christian Andersen

There was once an emperor who loved new clothes above everything else. Designers, tailors, clothmakers, dyers, and specialists in all sorts of needlework travelled to his city from all over the world. Anyone who could suggest flashy, fancy new outfits for the emperor was always very welcome at the palace.

One day, it was the turn of two weavers to be quickly ushered into the emperor's dressing room. The emperor, his butler and all his Officers of the Royal Wardrobe, gasped with amazement as they listened to them describe their work.

"We have created a special fabric that is so light and airy the wearer cannot feel it," the first weaver announced.

"Our samples are top secret, which is why we have not been able to bring any to show you," the second weaver explained.

"However we can assure you that not only are our designs and patterns exquisitely beautiful," said the first weaver, "but the fabric has the unique advantage that it is completely invisible to anyone who is not worthy of his job –"

"– or who is just plain stupid!" laughed the second weaver, and the emperor and all his courtiers gasped and chuckled along.

"We would be honoured if you would like to order the very first suit made out of this extraordinary fabric, your imperial majesty," said the first weaver, bowing low.

The emperor clapped his hands with delight.

"I'd like to place an order right away!" he commanded, and he gave the two weavers a large sum of money so that they could buy the rare, expensive materials they needed and begin their work without delay.

The weavers set up their looms in the palace studio and got going right away. News of the strange cloth spread round the city like wildfire and soon everyone was talking about it. But the weavers worked behind closed doors and no one got even a glimpse of what they were doing. Still, day and night everyone heard the looms clicking and the shuttles flying, and work on the magical cloth seemed to be progressing well.

As the days went on, the emperor began to feel rather uneasy about seeing the cloth for the first time. Imagine if I can't see the fabric myself! he thought to himself.

How dreadfully embarrassing that would be! The worried emperor decided to send his trusted old butler to see how the weavers were getting on. He was sure that his butler was both fit for his job and very wise, and would be sure to see the wonderful material.

The weavers bowed low and ushered the butler into the studio. But the butler couldn't see anything at all. Heavens above! the butler thought to himself. Those looms look totally bare to me! I must either be a very bad butler, or else I'm an idiot. No one must ever find out . . .

So he praised the material that he could not see, told the king that the weavers' work was indeed magnificent, and everyone in the city heard that the cloth was truly unbelievable!

Soon afterwards, the weavers sent word to the emperor that they needed more money to buy essential items for the work. The emperor had been so delighted with the butler's report that he sent them twice as much money as before. The emperor was more excited than ever. "I'm going to have the most amazing suit of clothes in the world!" he giggled to himself ten times a day.

Eventually, just as the impatient emperor thought he was going to explode with waiting, the weavers announced their work was finished. They went to the dressing room to present the material to the emperor amid fanfares of trumpets. "Is the cloth not beautiful beyond all imagining?" the weavers sighed.

The emperor smiled a wide smile, trying to hide his horror. All that the weavers appeared to be holding up before him was thin air. The emperor's worst fear had come true – to him the cloth was invisible! I cannot be thought to be a fool or not worthy to be ruler, the despairing emperor thought. So he beamed and leant forwards and inspected the air. "Wonderful! Splendid! Magnificent!" he cried, and his butler and all the Officers of the Royal Wardrobe nodded and cried out compliments. None of them could see anything either, but they weren't about to risk losing their jobs by admitting it.

So the weavers got out their tape measures and their scissors and they set about cutting the thin air (or so it seemed) into a pattern. All night long they sewed with needles which appeared to have no thread, and in the morning they announced that the emperor's new clothes were ready. "Now if your imperial majesty would care to disrobe, we will dress you in the amazing garments."

The emperor swallowed hard and took off all his clothes. The weavers helped him on with the underpants and trousers and shirt and jacket that he couldn't see.

"Aren't they lighter than cobwebs?" they sighed. The emperor spluttered his agreement. He couldn't feel that he had any clothes on at all.

The emperor stood back and looked at himself in the mirror. According to what he saw, he didn't have a stitch on! But he turned this way and that, pretending to admire himself. And the butler and all the Officers of the Royal Wardrobe cried out, "How wonderfully the new clothes fit you, sire!" and "We have never seen the like of the amazing colours!" and "The design is a work of genius!" – even though it looked to them as if the emperor was as naked as the day he was born.

Everyone else can see my new suit except me, the emperor thought to himself glumly. And he walked out of the palace to parade before the people in his marvellous new clothes.

The streets were lined with hundreds of men and women who ooohed! and aaaahed! over the emperor's invisible new clothes – for none of them wanted to admit that they couldn't see them.

Suddenly, a little boy's shrill voice rose over the applause of the crowd. "But the emperor has nothing on!" the child shouted. "Nothing on at all!" Suddenly there was a stunned silence and the little boy found that hundreds of pairs of eyes were staring at him. Then someone sniggered . . . someone else tried to stifle a giggle . . . another person guffawed and snorted . . . and the whole crowd burst out into uncontrollable peals of laughter.

The emperor's face turned as red as a ripe tomato. "I am indeed a fool!" he murmured. "I have been swindled by two tricksters!" He ran back to the palace as fast as his short, naked legs could carry him – but the clever (and now very rich) weavers were long gone!

The Little Mermaid

retold from the original tale by Hans Christian Andersen

F ar, far out in the ocean, the water is as blue as cornflowers and deeper than the tallest mountain. It is there that the sea-people live, and in the very deepest waters lies the Sea King's palace of coral and mother-of-pearl. The Sea King's beloved wife had died, so his mother, the old queen, took care of his six beautiful mermaid daughters. All day long, the princesses sang and danced, swimming in and out of the pillars and halls of the palace. Sometimes shy, brightly coloured fish swam up to eat out of their hands. And at other times, each would tend the little garden that she cared for in the royal grounds.

Each mermaid princess gave her garden its own particular style and design: one was shaped like a whale; another had a rockery of shells; yet another had flowerbeds where the sea-horses came to graze. But the youngest mermaid's garden was shaped like the sun that shone on the world above the sea, and the flowers that grew there blazed red and orange and yellow like the sunlight.

The little mermaid had never been up to the ocean's surface and seen the upper world, for the princesses were only allowed to do so when they reached fifteen years old. But the little mermaid longed for that day to come. She loved to hear the stories her grandmother told of people and ships and cities and animals and meadows and forests and the like. And many a night the little mermaid stood at her open chamber window, peering up at the watery reflections of the moon and the stars and the dark shapes of ships as they passed like clouds above her.

When each of
her sisters came of
age, the little
mermaid begged them
eagerly to tell her
everything they had seen.
Then at last, she turned
fifteen and it was her turn to see
the upper world for herself.

The little mermaid thought it was more beautiful
than she had ever imagined. Her head broke through the
foam when the sun had just gone down and the clouds
looked as if they were on fire with red and gold. The sound
of music and singing was coming from a tall-masted ship
bedecked all about with coloured flags and banners.
Suddenly rockets zoomed up from it into the sky which
exploded into stars that fell glittering all around her – the

little mermaid had never seen fireworks before. When she
was lifted up on the swell of the sea, she saw onto the ship's
magnificent deck and understood the reason for the
wonderful celebrations: it was the birthday party of a prince,
more handsome than any merman she had ever seen.

As the little mermaid gazed with delight at the
prince and his ship, she heard a familiar rumbling stirring
deep within the sea. A storm was coming! All at once the
sky darkened. Sheets of rain lashed the ship. The waves
towered into mountains that hurled the ship upwards and
sent it crashing down towards the depths. The little
mermaid saw with alarm that the ship wouldn't be able to
hold out against the might of the weather and the ocean,
and she ducked under the waves as wooden planks and
other pieces of the ship came flying out of the darkness at
her head. Through the murky waters, the little mermaid
was horrified to see human bodies come floating down

around her – and among them
was her beautiful prince,
choking and gasping for air.

The little mermaid shot
through the water and clutched him close to her, and
began swimming up to the light until his head was above
water. The little mermaid hauled the exhausted prince to
the shore and let the waves wash him onto the sand, and
she stayed in the foam and watched him until the storm
had died away and the morning sunlight came streaming
warmly through the clouds. Then she saw the green hills
for the first time and heard the peal of bells, and she saw a
group of young girls come skipping out of a white building
with a cross on the top. One of the girls noticed the prince
where he lay. She ran to him and laid his head in her lap,
and slowly the prince opened his eyes. He looked up at the
girl and smiled, and the little mermaid turned away sadly,

for she knew the prince thought it was that girl who had rescued him. Down, down, down, the little mermaid dived into the deeps – and her heart ached all the way back to her father's palace.

From that moment on, the little mermaid was thoughtful and sad. She longed to see her handsome prince again, to tell him that she loved him and wanted to be with him forever. She wanted to be human more than anything else in the whole world. There was only one thing she could do: make the dangerous journey to the cold, dark depths of the ocean to see the Water-Witch.

The Water-Witch's lair was set about with the skeletons of humans she had drowned and the remains of ships she had wrecked. The little mermaid trembled with fear as she explained why she had come.

"What you long for is extremely difficult to give," the Water-Witch cackled.

"I can make your
tail disappear and
give you legs so that
you can walk about
with the humans in
the world above. But
every step you take will be
as painful as if you are treading on knives. And I cannot
make your prince fall in love with you. It is up to you, and
you alone, to do that. If your prince marries another, the
morning afterwards your heart will break and you will
turn to foam on the water."

The little mermaid shuddered, but she bade the
Water-Witch continue.

"The price for such strong magic is very high," spat
the witch. "Once I have given you legs, there is no
changing your mind. You will never be able to return to

the sea as a mermaid to see your family . . . And there is one more thing. I cannot mix the potion you need unless you give me your voice."

The little mermaid longed so badly for her prince and for a human soul that she whispered, "So be it." The words were the last sounds she ever uttered. For then the Water-Witch took the little mermaid's voice and brewed up an evil-smelling potion for her in exchange.

The little mermaid felt as if her heart would break with grief as she swam back past her father's palace, leaving her sleeping family for the world above. She splashed onto the sand, half-choking through her tears and half-gasping for air, and looked at her beautiful silvery fishtail for the last time. Then the little mermaid raised the witch's brew to her lips and drank deeply. At once pain wracked her body and she fell into a dead faint . . .

The little mermaid awoke to find her handsome

prince standing over her, looking worried. "Are you all right?" he asked, but the little mermaid couldn't reply. Instead, she smiled as she looked down at her body and saw that she had the prettiest pair of legs she could have wished for. Falteringly, she stood up for the very first time. The little mermaid put out her foot – and it was true, each step was like treading on knives. But soon she was dancing and running and skipping along the beach for joy, and the prince was utterly enchanted.

The prince took his new little friend back to the palace and dressed her in fine robes of silk and satin. He didn't seem to mind that she was dumb, and kept her by his side at all times, calling her "my beautiful little foundling".

Yet although the little mermaid was happier than she had ever dreamed was possible, there was a sadness in her eyes and a heaviness in her heart. Each night, she would creep out of the palace and go down to the seashore. Sometimes she saw her sisters way out among the surf, and they would sing to her sadly as they floated on the waves. Once, she even thought she glimpsed the golden crowns of her father and grandmother – but perhaps it was just the moonlight glinting on the water.

Eventually a day came when the prince led the little mermaid onto a fine ship just like the one from which she had rescued him. They sailed for a night and a day, and all the time the little mermaid longed to leap into the waves and dive down to see her family far below. The ship finally arrived in the harbour of a neighbouring kingdom, and all the people lined the streets to meet them, waving flags and cheering. "See how they welcome me," the prince whispered to the little mermaid. "For today I am going to marry their princess."

The little mermaid felt as if someone had grabbed her heart with icy fingers. Surely it couldn't be true? But when the prince's bride came running down the palace steps to meet him, the little mermaid understood. It was the girl who had found him on the beach; the girl whom the prince thought had saved him from the sea; the girl whom the prince thought was the little mermaid.

That afternoon, the little mermaid stood in church

dressed in silk and gold, holding the bride's train. And all the way back to the ship, she cried silent, dry tears.

That night, as the splendid ship floated on the waves, there were flags and fireworks and music and dancing – and the little mermaid felt no more a part of the celebrations than she had when she had watched the prince's birthday party from afar.

The little mermaid stood on the deck all night and listened to the sighing of the sea. She felt the warm night wind on her face and her hair floated in the damp sea mists. When the first rays of the dawn lit up the horizon, the little mermaid prepared herself to dissolve into foam on the waves. But instead, she saw transparent beings of light flying to her through the air. They lifted her up on their wings and soared off into the sky, and the little mermaid found that she was one of them. "We are the daughters of the air," the beautiful beings explained.

"We do not have an immortal soul, but if we perform enough acts of goodness and kindness, we will one day win one for ourselves. And this is your reward for the suffering you have endured."

The little mermaid raised her hands towards the sun and the tears in her eyes were tears of joy. She looked down upon the prince and his bride on their ship. They were searching for her sadly in the water, thinking she had fallen overboard. But the little mermaid didn't stay to watch them for long. She blew them a kiss and flew onwards with the daughters of the air.

The Golden Touch

a myth from Ancient Greece

There was once a king called Midas who loved gold more than anything in the world. Each day, he spent hour after hour in his treasure house, running his hands through his sacks of gold coins, admiring his golden jars and statues, and holding up his golden jewellery to the light to watch it gleam and shine. Midas thought that the precious metal was a much more delightful colour than the emerald green of the grass or the sapphire blue of the sea. He thought it was far more beautiful than the gold of waving fields of wheat, the gold of his wife's hair – even the gold of sunshine.

The king once helped the god Dionysus by taking care of one of his friends who was lost. Dionysus was very grateful and insisted, "Let me repay you for your kindness by granting you a wish! Now think hard . . . Make it something good! . . . Whatever you like . . ."

Midas knew exactly what he wanted. "I wish for everything I touch to turn to gold!" he declared.

"Are you sure about that?" Dionysus asked. "Are you quite, quite sure?"

"What could be better?" cried Midas, delightedly.

"Very well then," sighed the god. "It is done."

Midas couldn't wait to try out his new powers. He hurried over to a tree and snapped off a twig. Unbelievable! It immediately grew heavy and bright. It had turned to solid gold. Joyfully, Midas rushed around touching everything in his royal garden. Soon the apples hung on the trees like golden baubles. The flowers

hardened into gold sculptures. The
fountain froze into a spray of golden
glitter and the grass solidified into a
gold pavement.

"How wonderful!" laughed
Midas, clapping his hands. "Now
for my palace!" and he picked up
his robes and ran inside. By the time Midas reached the
cool of his great chamber, his clothes had stiffened into a
fabric woven from pure gold thread. "Ooof!" puffed Midas.
"That's a little heavy!" The weight of his golden clothes
were dragging him down, slowing him up and making his
shoulders ache. Still, thought Midas, that's a minor
botheration compared to how beautiful my robes now
look! He set off through the halls and corridors, touching
pillars, pictures, doors, furniture, floors . . . until everything
glowed gold.

Phew! It was hungry, thirsty work! Midas sank into one of his new golden chairs at his new golden dining table and called for his servants to bring him his lunch. He wriggled about a bit on his rock hard seat, but couldn't get comfy. "Never mind!" said Midas to himself, as the servants brought in platter after platter of delicious food. "I don't know any other king who is rich enough to eat off gold plates!" And he touched each serving dish and bowl and saw them gleam.

"Amazing!" Midas whooped, and licking his lips, he reached for a juicy chicken leg. "OWWW!" he yelled, biting down on hard metal and breaking a tooth. He reached for a goblet of wine and took a gulp. "AAARRGH!" Midas roared, as the mouthful of gold got stuck in his throat. The king pushed his chair back, spitting out the hunk of treasure.

"Oh, no!" the king moaned. Suddenly he realised

what the god Dionysus had been trying to warn him about. "I'm going to have a whole kingdom full of gold, but I'm not going to be able to eat or drink anything!"

At that very moment, Midas's golden doors swung open and his little daughter came running towards him. Midas backed away in horror – but it was too late. "Daddy!" the little girl cried, flinging her arms happily around him. Suddenly the king's beloved daughter was no more than a lifeless statue. Midas howled with misery and huge tears began to stream from his eyes. "I would gladly give away every piece of gold that I own to have my little girl back again," he wailed. "How foolish I have been! There must be some way to take back my wish!"

Desperately trying not to touch anything else, Midas hurried to Dionysus and begged him to undo his magic. "Go and wash in the River Pactolus," the god instructed him. As soon as the king had done so, he was hugely relieved to find that his golden touch was gone. All the things Midas had turned into gold were back to normal – including his beautiful little daughter. After that, if the king had had his way, he would never have looked at another nugget of gold as long as he lived. But the god Dionysus turned the sandy bed of the River Pactolus gold for ever more, so that every time Midas walked along its banks, he would remember his greedy mistake.

The Nutcracker Prince

retold from the original tale by Ernst Hoffmann

D r Drosselmeier was an old man with a secret. In his youth, he had been the most nimble-fingered, highly skilled craftsman in the entire royal court.

Dr Drosselmeier had made clocks that were mechanical wonders. Some chimed with a hundred tinkling bells. Others were decorated with tiny musicians that danced and played their instruments as they struck the hour. Some even had secret doors, out of which little birds fluttered and flew around the room, chirruping the passing minutes. Yes, Dr Drosselmeier's clocks had been the talk

of the palace.

But the most amazing thing he had ever made was a mouse-trap.

Dr Drosselmeier had invented a brilliant clockwork trap that caught mice in their hundreds, twenty-four hours a day. Everyone in the palace had been delighted – except for the Mouse King. He too had lived in the palace with his subjects. Now, he was forced to leave and find another home, and he was furious about it. The Mouse King knew powerful magic and he took his revenge on Dr Drosselmeier by turning his nephew into an ugly, wooden doll.

The doll wore a painted soldier's uniform and it had a prince's crown painted mockingly onto its head, and its jaws moved so it could crack nuts between its teeth. The Mouse King's spell was so strong that there was only one way to undo it. Firstly, the nutcracker prince had somehow to kill the evil Mouse King. And secondly, a little girl had to love him, in spite of his ugliness. Well, Dr Drosselmeier had no idea where the Mouse King had gone, and he certainly didn't know a little girl kind enough to take pity on the poor, ugly wooden doll. And so his nephew had stayed a nutcracker.

From that moment on, Dr Drosselmeier had never made another clock. He lost all heart for mechanical things and so he lost his job at the palace, too. Dr Drosselmeier blamed himself entirely for his nephew's dreadful disappearance and he had never breathed a word of what had happened to anyone. But ever since, he had been trying to find a way to break the Mouse King's spell . . . and at last, he thought he had.

Dr Drosselmeier's goddaughter, Clara, had grown into the kindest little girl anyone could wish to meet. If any little girl was going to take pity on the stiff, glaring nutcracker prince, it would be Clara.

Now it was Christmas Eve, and Dr Drosselmeier had arrived at Clara's house trembling with excitement. He wasn't excited because there was a party going on with games and music and dancing. No, Dr Drosselmeier was excited because tonight was the night he hoped the evil magic would be undone and his nephew would return to life.

While the party guests talked and joked and laughed together, Dr Drosselmeier set about emptying the huge bag he had brought with him. It was filled with gingerbread and shortcake, candy walking sticks and sugar

pigs, nuts and bon bons, nougat
and humbugs . . . High and low,
in every corner of the room,
Dr Drosselmeier heaped piles
of all the Mouse King's
favourite things to eat. That
should tempt him out from wherever

he's hiding, thought Dr Drosselmeier, determinedly.

Then it was time to give Clara her Christmas
present. The little girl's eyes opened wide with excitement
as she stripped off the sparkly paper. But her face suddenly
fell as she saw the ugly nutcracker prince. Then, gently,
Clara stroked the doll's face. He wasn't cute, he wasn't
cuddly – he wasn't even new! But that was exactly why
Clara decided she loved him. She couldn't bear to think of
leaving him all alone, laughed at and unloved – especially
at Christmas time. Clara clutched the nutcracker prince

close to her and hugged him tight. And Dr Drosselmeier slipped away from the party, his heart light with hope . . .

When the party was over and it was bedtime at last, Clara tucked the wooden doll up next to her. "I love you," she whispered, just before she fell asleep. "I'll look after you always." And that night, Clara had a very strange dream. She dreamt that the nutcracker prince woke up beside her. He smiled at Clara and held her hand, and led her downstairs. There was scuffling and squeaking coming from the drawing room, and when Clara peeped around the door she saw a terrible sight. There were mice everywhere! They were climbing all over Dr Drosselmeier's goodies, fighting and biting to get at the sweets. And worst of all, a horrible seven-headed mouse was standing in the middle of the carpet, cackling with glee at all the arguing and the mess. The seven-headed mouse wore seven gold crowns and Clara could tell he must be the king of the evil creatures.

Very bravely, the
nutcracker prince charged at
the gruesome Mouse King
with a sword glinting in his
hand and began to fight
furiously. But he was completely
outnumbered. The mice swarmed to
their king's defence. They dragged
the nutcracker prince to the ground
and he disappeared under a
thousand biting, clawing bodies.
Just as the Mouse King threw
back his head and began to laugh,
Clara tore her slipper off her foot and threw it at him with
all her might. WHAM! It hit the Mouse King on four of
his seven horrible heads. He staggered to and fro for a
second, and then collapsed dead to the floor.

As soon as the mice saw that their leader was no more, their courage deserted them. They hurried to scoop up his body and then they were gone, streaming off through cracks in the wall, holes in the skirting and gaps in the floorboards.

The nutcracker prince ran to Clara and kissed her. "Thank you for all you have done for me," he whispered, and there were tears sparkling in his painted eyes. "Let me repay you by taking you on a wonderful journey to my kingdom, the realm of sweets . . ."

It was the most wonderful dream Clara had ever had. She travelled through forests made of barley sugar, crossed rivers that ran with lemonade, picked flowers of sherbert, walked on paths of chocolate, and visited the nutcracker prince's gingerbread castle. In fact, Clara was very sorry to be woken up – even though it was Christmas Day itself! She hugged the wooden doll and told him,

"You're the best present I've ever had," and she could have sworn that his smile was even broader than usual.

Meanwhile, across the city, Dr Drosselmeier had also woken up to find the best present he'd ever had. There sprawled underneath his Christmas tree, sleeping an exhausted but peaceful sleep, was his brave, handsome nephew . . .

The Sword in the Stone

a Celtic legend

The blacksmith's anvil had suddenly appeared in the courtyard of the cathedral on Christmas morning. No one knew how it had got there. The anvil had a sword stuck into it and stood on a huge stone. Words were carved right round it which read: Whoever pulls out this sword is the rightful king of the Britons.

Many a proud lord had stepped up and tried to pull the sword out of the mysterious anvil. But even though they had heaved and sweated and grunted and pulled and pulled and pulled, all of them had walked away disappointed. Now almost a week had passed. It was time for the New Year's Eve jousting festival, and still the anvil stood on the stone in the courtyard with the sword sticking out of it.

Every year, bold knights came to the capital city from all over the kingdom to ride against each other in the New Year's Eve jousting festival and show off how brave they were. This year, Sir Ector's son, Sir Kay, would joust for the very first time. Sir Ector's younger son, Arthur, was going along too, as Sir Kay's squire. Sir Ector and his sons lived in the very furthest corner of the kingdom – so far away from the capital city that news of the strange anvil hadn't even reached them. It took them three days of hard riding until they saw the towering cathedral spire and the bright fluttering flags of the jousting field in the distance. Then a dreadful thing happened. Sir Kay put his hand down by his side to pat his trusty sword – and there was nothing there. "My sword!" Sir Kay gasped. "It's gone!"

Arthur turned quite pale with horror. It was a squire's job to make sure that a knight was properly equipped. "We must have left it at the lodging house we stayed at last night," he groaned. "Don't worry, Kay. I'll dash back and fetch it." Before anyone could argue, Arthur had wheeled his horse around and was galloping at full tilt back down the road. There wasn't a second to lose.

But when Arthur arrived back at the lodging house, there wasn't a sign of Sir Kay's sword anywhere. Arthur raced his horse back to the city wondering how on earth he was going to break the bad news to his brother. He was very nearly at the jousting field when he galloped past the cathedral courtyard and saw the sword sticking out of the magical anvil on the stone. Arthur reined in his panting horse at once and looked all around him. There was no one about; everyone was at the jousting competition. It certainly didn't look as if the sword would be missed if he borrowed it for a while. "I promise I'll bring it back later," Arthur muttered out loud to no one in particular. He dashed over the snow, jumped up onto the stone and grasped the sword. It slid out of the anvil as easily as a needle pulls through cloth. "Gadzooks!" Arthur breathed, as he gazed at the mighty, jewelled blade in his hands. "This is the most magnificent weapon I have ever seen!" Then he remembered that the competition was about to begin. He sprinted back to his horse, leapt into the saddle, and arrived at the jousting field just as the first fanfares were being trumpeted.

Sir Kay was astonished at the superb weapon that

his younger brother handed him. He and his father had just heard all about the mysterious anvil from the other knights at the jousting competition, and he realised at once where the strange sword must have come from. "See, father!" he cried over the crowds, brandishing the sword over his head. "I must be the new king of the Britons!"

Sir Ector came running at once and gasped at the magnificent weapon in Kay's hands. "How have you got this?" he demanded.

Kay's face fell. "Arthur brought it to me," he mumbled.

Sir Ector's face was grave. "Who pulled this out of the stone and gave it to you?" he quizzed Arthur.

"N-n-o one," stammered Arthur. Quite a few people had gathered around by now, pointing and shouting and staring, and suddenly he felt very nervous. "I pulled it out of the stone myself. I was going to put it back when Kay had finished with it, honest!"

Sir Ector led Arthur back to
the cathedral and into the
courtyard, with a huge and
excited crowd following hot on
their heels. "Put the sword back
where you found it, son," he
told Arthur.

"All right," shrugged Arthur.
He climbed onto the stone and
thrust the sword back into the
anvil.

First, Sir Ector himself tried
to pull it out. Then Sir Kay heaved at
it with all his might. The sword didn't budge an inch.

"Now show us how you did it, son," said Sir Ector,
his voice trembling slightly.

Everyone held their breath as Arthur stepped up to the anvil. As he pulled the sword out effortlessly, the cheer that went up could be heard all over the capital city and beyond.

And that is how a young boy called Arthur, who wasn't even a knight, was crowned king of the Britons and eventually became the greatest of all the heroes who ever lived in the Celtic lands.

Ricky with the Tuft

retold from the original story by Charles Perrault

Aaaarrggh!" cried the queen, as she saw her newborn son for the first time. "Surely this baby can't be mine! He's hideously ugly!"

The fairy midwife sighed. It was true. The tiny face of the queen's new baby boy was swamped by a huge red nose. He was cross-eyed and his shoulders were humped. One of his legs was much shorter than the other. And to top it all, the baby was totally bald except for a single tuft of hair sticking up in the middle of his head. "Never mind your little boy's looks, your majesty," the fairy midwife comforted the queen. "I promise that your son will grow up to be far more intelligent, witty and charming than other people, and everyone will love him for it. What's more, I'm going to give him a gift. I'm going to give him the power to make the girl he falls in love with as intelligent as he is, so he won't ever get bored with her company . . . Now, what are you going to call your special little son?"

"Ricky . . ." the queen decided, making up her mind that she loved her son after all. "He's my little Ricky with the Tuft."

Not long afterwards, the queen of a neighbouring kingdom gave birth to twin daughters. The first tiny girl to be born was so perfect that the queen at first thought she was looking at a little angel from heaven. But the second baby was as ugly as her elder sister was beautiful.

"Oh dear," said the fairy midwife – the same one who had helped at the birth of Ricky with the Tuft. "I have to tell you that your elder daughter will grow up to be incredibly stupid . . . However, there is some comfort. Your younger daughter will stay ugly, but she will be so clever that no one will even notice."

The queen was relieved that her younger daughter's fate seemed to be taken care of, but she was very worried about her elder daughter. "Can't we somehow give the elder one some of the younger one's intelligence?" the queen suggested.

"I'm afraid that's beyond my powers," the fairy midwife replied. "However, what I can do for her is to make her more beautiful than any girl in the world. What's more, I'll also give her a gift. The boy she falls in love with will become as beautiful as she is, so she'll never tire of looking at him."

Sixteen or so years passed, and the two princesses grew up exactly as the fairy midwife had said they would.

Strangers were at first entranced by the beauty of the elder princess. However, they would soon creep away because trying to make conversation with her was as difficult as digging a field with a spoon. The strangers would then turn to the younger princess and be captivated by her intelligent and entertaining chat. Everyone totally forgot how plain and ungainly the princess was after only five minutes in her enchanting company.

Unfortunately, the beautiful elder sister knew very well that she was exceedingly stupid and embarrassing. She often stole away into the woods to be on her own – and it was on one of these lonely walks that she first encountered Ricky with the Tuft.

It wasn't an accident that the princess and the prince came to meet each other. Ricky with the Tuft had fallen desperately in love with the pictures of the princess that were for sale in all the shops. After collecting every single one, sticking them all over his bedroom walls, and gazing at them adoringly for hours on end, Ricky with the Tuft had decided that he wanted to marry the real thing. He had set off determined to find her.

"My lady, I feel as if I have been looking for you all my life," sighed Ricky with the Tuft, bowing low to the princess.

The princess just shrugged, as she couldn't think of anything to say to the remarkably ugly prince who stood before her.

"I have never seen a girl as beautiful as you," admitted Ricky with the Tuft. "And as I should know more than most, beauty is an important blessing that shouldn't be taken for granted."

The sad princess blurted out, "I would much rather be as ugly as you are, if only I could be a little less stupid!"

Luckily, Ricky with the Tuft wasn't offended. "I have the perfect solution," he smiled. "I love you with all my heart, and if you will only consent to be my wife, you will become as wise and witty as you could ever wish to be."

The princess wasn't sure if she understood or not what the prince was saying. She stood gaping open-mouthed.

"I can see you are a little taken aback by the suddenness of my proposal," said Ricky with the Tuft, kindly. "So I will give you a whole year to get used to the idea."

The princess said nothing to disagree, and so Ricky with the Tuft trotted off home, his heart full to bursting with happiness.

From that moment on, the princess discovered that she was as intelligent and entertaining as she was beautiful. The news spread rapidly, and princes and lords and earls came from kingdoms far and wide to seek her hand in marriage. Of course, in all the excitement, the princess quite forgot about Ricky with the Tuft. Her mind was completely taken up with one big worry. The princess thought each suitor very handsome in his own way, but now that she herself was so clever, she found them all extremely boring! "How can I marry a man whose conversation sends me to sleep within five minutes?" she sighed wistfully.

One day, the princess decided to wander alone into the woods to think the problem over. She hadn't been gone long when she came across a hundred servants preparing a banquet among the trees. They were hanging flags and balloons and coloured lanterns in the branches; they were scurrying to and fro in a vast outdoor kitchen, cooking a delicious feast; they were setting up a dance floor and a bandstand, and laying thousands of tables and chairs – all beautifully decked with flowers. "Whatever is going on?" the astounded princess asked one of the servants. She had attended many wonderful balls, but had never been to one on such a grand, gorgeous scale.

"The person giving this banquet must have a very important reason to throw such a wonderful party."

"Tomorrow our master, Ricky with the Tuft, is getting married," the breathless servant replied. "He loves his bride with all his heart and is throwing the best wedding feast ever!"

The princess gasped as she suddenly remembered the squinting, limping, hunchbacked prince with the huge nose and the strange tuft of hair, whom she had met exactly a year before. I gave him the impression I would marry him! she thought in horror.

The princess suddenly saw Ricky with the Tuft himself heading through the trees towards her. "Good afternoon, my darling," he cried. "I have kept my word and have come to see how you feel about marrying me now."

The princess hung her head in shame. "There is no doubt in my mind that you are the kindest, most honourable, most intelligent person in the world," she sobbed. "I would love to be with you forever – but I can't! I am deeply sorry that I can never marry you, for I can't get over your terrible ugliness!"

To the princess's amazement, Ricky with the Tuft laughed out loud. "Well, I do believe that you've fallen in love with me after all," he cried. And when the princess looked up, she saw that Ricky with the Tuft had become as handsome as she herself was beautiful. "Didn't you know you had the power to do that?" the prince beamed.

The princess fell into his arms, and the very next day, she and her prince had the best wedding feast ever – just as Ricky with the Tuft had wanted.

The Happy Prince

retold from the original tale by Oscar Wilde

The statue of the Happy Prince stood high up above the city on a tall column. He glittered in the sunlight, for he was painted all over in gold leaf and had a glowing ruby set into his sword hilt and two sparkling sapphires for eyes. The people of the city often looked up at the Happy Prince and sighed, for they admired his beauty and envied his contented smile.

One evening, a little swallow came fluttering through the skies and landed between the prince's golden feet. It was well past the end of the summer and the wind had grown chill. The swallow's friends had set off several

weeks ago for a warmer land.
The swallow had stayed
behind because he had
fallen in love with a slender
reed by the river, and he
could not bear to leave her.

But the wind had grown chill and
the bite of frost had crept into the air. The shivering
swallow had realised that to stay any longer would mean
certain death from the cold. He had begged the reed to
travel with him, but the reed had simply shaken her head.
So the swallow had been forced to fly sadly off without
her. Tomorrow he would fly away and catch up with his
friends. Now the little bird tucked his head under his wing
and prepared to get some rest for the long journey. But
just as the swallow began to drift off into dreams, large
raindrops started to fall on his head. The swallow looked

up in puzzlement at the clear night sky and saw that the statue above him was crying.

"Who are you and why are you weeping?" the little swallow asked, as the statue's tears shone in the moonlight like diamonds.

"People call me the Happy Prince," replied the statue, "but in truth, I am full of sadness. They have set me up here so high that I can look out over the whole city and see all its ugliness and misery. Tonight, I can see a poor woman sitting in a house near the edge of town. The woman is thin from hunger and pale from tiredness, but she is still at work, sewing passion-flowers onto a gown for one of the queen's maids-of-honour. In the corner of the room, her little boy lies very ill in bed, asking for oranges. But the woman has no money to buy him anything, so all she can give him is water." The Happy Prince sighed. "Little swallow, will you pluck out the ruby from my sword

and take it to
the woman, so that
she might sell it to the
jeweller for money? My feet are
fastened to this pedestal and I cannot move."

The Happy Prince looked so sad that the swallow agreed to be his messenger. The little bird pecked the ruby out of the prince's sword and flew away with it in his beak over the rooftops. He flew in at the window of the woman's house and found her slumped over her work in a worn-out sleep. The swallow laid the jewel down next to her thimble, then he flew gently round the bed, fanning the feverish, sick boy with his wings until he looked much cooler and more comfortable. Then the swallow flew back to the Happy Prince and told him what he had done. "It's strange," the bird remarked. "I feel a warm glow inside me, even though the weather is so cold."

"That is because you have done a good deed," explained the Happy Prince, as the tired little swallow closed his eyes.

Next day, the swallow flew all over the city bidding goodbye to everyone and everything. "I am leaving tonight for Egypt!" he cried. But when in the evening he came to say farewell to the Happy Prince, he found that the statue was crying once again.

"Far across the city I can see into an attic where a young man leans over a desk. He is struggling to finish a play for the Director of the Theatre, but he is too cold to write anymore. His fire has died away and he has no

money to buy either wood or any food for his supper."
A glistening tear rolled off the end of the Happy Prince's
nose and sploshed onto the swallow's head. "Little swallow,
will you stay with me one more night and be my
messenger? Will you pluck out one of my sapphire eyes
and take it to him?"

"Dear prince," said the swallow, "I will not pluck out
your eye." and tears gleamed in his own.

"Little swallow, please do as I ask," begged the
Happy Prince, and he looked so sad that the swallow
fluttered up and plucked out one of his sapphire eyes and
flew away with it to the young man in the attic. The little
swallow was very relieved when he returned to nestle at
the Happy Prince's feet, for the air underneath his wings
had really become very cold indeed.

The next day, the swallow flew down to the harbour
and watched all the big ships sailing away to lands where

the breezes were warm and the days were long. "I am leaving too, tonight!" he sang out to everyone he saw. At sunset, the swallow flew off to the Happy Prince to say goodbye. "In the square below," said the Happy Prince, "I can see a little matchgirl whose matches have all spilled into the gutter. She is crying because she can make no money and if she goes home empty-handed, her father will beat her." The Happy Prince smiled sadly. "Little swallow, pluck out my other eye and take it to the little matchgirl so she can be happy."

"But then you will be blind!" cried the swallow.

"Little swallow, please do as I ask," whispered the Happy Prince, and he looked so sad that the bird did as he wanted.

"Now you can no longer see," the little swallow said, as he fluttered back to the statue. "I will stay with you always."

"But little swallow," protested the Happy Prince, "your friends will be waiting for you on the hazy banks of the River Nile."

"I will stay with you always and be your eyes," the swallow promised, and he slept between the prince's feet.

Next day, the swallow flew all over the city and told the Happy Prince what he had seen there. "I have seen the rich making merry in their beautiful houses while beggars lie outside their gates," the swallow murmured. "I have seen old people who sit all day on their own, cold and lonely. I have seen small children tremble in front of bullies. I have seen much suffering and misery."

"Little swallow," said the prince, "with your beak, peel off the fine gold that covers me. Fly with leaves of it to all the poor people of my city."

The little swallow sighed, but did what he was told. Then the statue of the Happy Prince was dull and grey.

As the faithful bird finally settled down between his friend's feet, the snow began to fall in thick white flakes. The streets glistened silver with a lining of frost. Icicles hung like shards of glass from the rooftops. And the little swallow shivered at the foot of the Happy Prince. He tried beating his wings to keep warm, but eventually he knew that he was going to die. The little swallow used his last drop of strength to flutter up to the prince's shoulder. "Goodbye, Happy Prince," he cried. "I will not see you again."

"I am glad you are finally going to where the sun will warm your wings," the Happy Prince said.

"I am not going to Egypt," murmured the swallow,

"I am going to sleep forever." And he kissed the Happy Prince on the lips and fell down dead at his feet.

That very moment, a strange cracking noise came from within the Happy Prince. It was so loud that the Mayor heard it way down below. He peered up at the statue for the first time in months. "Good lord!" he remarked. "However did the Happy Prince get that shabby? We'll have to replace him with something else."

The very next day, workmen pulled down the Happy Prince from his column and threw him into a furnace. They cleared away the dead swallow and then put a statue of the Mayor on the column instead. But the Happy Prince knew nothing about all this, because his heart had broken. In fact, when the workmen opened the door of the furnace, they saw his cracked lead heart for themselves, because it would not melt away. They threw it onto the same rubbish dump on which they had thrown the dead swallow was lying. And when God asked his angels to bring him the two most precious things in all the city, they took the Happy Prince's heart and the little swallow with them up to heaven.

Wizards and Witches, Giants and Genies

Amal and the Genie

A Persian fairytale

Many moons ago in ancient Persia there lived a bright young man called Amal. He was out one day when he had the misfortune to meet a genie. Now sometimes genies can be good news, but this one was in a very bad temper and he was looking for trouble. Amal had to think very quickly. He had no weapons with him, only an egg and a lump of salt in his pocket.

The genie came whirling up to Amal, but before he could say anything, Amal yelled at him.

"Genie! You and I should have a competition to see who is the strongest!"

You might think this was very foolish of Amal, but he knew two things about genies. One was that it is always better to take control first, and the second was that genies are not terribly bright. They are fine at conjuring up gorgeous palaces and flying carpets, but they are a bit slow when it comes to basic common sense.

Well, the genie looked at Amal, and then he laughed and laughed. It was not a nice sound, but Amal was not daunted.

"Hah! You don't look very strong," sniggered the genie. "I shall win this contest easily," and he laughed again.

Amal picked up a stone.

"You must squeeze this stone until water comes out of it," he said, handing the genie the stone.

Well, the genie squeezed and squeezed, and huffed and puffed, but, of course, no water came out of the stone. He threw it down in a temper.

"Not possible!" he snapped.

Amal bent down and picked up the stone, and squeezed. And with a scrunching sound, liquid ran down Amal's fingers. The genie was astonished. And so would you have been if you had been there. What clever Amal had done was to put the egg in the same hand as the stone, and it was the egg that was broken.

Genies are not terribly bright and this one was no exception.

Then Amal said, "Well, I win that one. But now perhaps you could crumble this stone into powder," and he handed the genie another stone. Well, the genie squeezed and squeezed, and huffed and puffed, but, of course, the stone did not crumble at all, not even the tiniest bit. The genie threw it down in a temper.

Amal picked it up and squeezed. And as he squeezed, powder fell from his fingers with a grinding sound. The genie was astonished. And so would you have been if you had been there, but you can guess what clever Amal had done. He put the salt in his hand as well as the stone.

The genie was feeling that his reputation was somewhat dented by Amal's performance so he needed to get his own back.

"You are clearly a great and mighty fighter," the genie said to Amal. "I should like to give you a meal to celebrate your achievements. Come and stay the night with me," and he smiled.

But Amal saw the smile, and kept his wits about him. After a dreadful meal (the genie was not a very good cook

either) they both lay down to sleep in the genie's cave.
Once Amal was sure the genie was asleep, he moved to the
other side of the cave, leaving his pillow in the bed to look
as if he were still there asleep. Then he watched. As the first
light of dawn filtered into the cave, the genie woke up. He
picked up a huge club and crept over to where he thought
Amal was lying, and he pounded the club down onto the
bed, seven times in all. Then he stomped
out of the cave to fetch some water
for his morning tea.

You can imagine his utter
dismay when, on returning,
he found Amal singing to
himself
as he lit the fire.

"Good morning, genie! I
thought I would get breakfast

ready," said Amal cheerfully. "I hope you slept better than I did," he continued. "Some wretched insect batted me in the face in the night, seven times in all."

Well, at this the genie gave a great shriek and whistled himself as fast as possible into an old oil lamp that lay on the floor of the cave. He wasn't seen again for hundreds and hundreds of years until a young lad called Aladdin happened to find the lamp. But that is another story, isn't it?

The Giant who Counted Carrots

a German fairytale

Hile igh upon a mountainside there was once a
giant who was always very sleepy, and when
he went to sleep, he would sleep for hundreds
of years at a time. So every time he awoke things had
changed a great deal. He spent time as a herdsman, but he
did not like being poor. So he went back to sleep. On
another visit he spent time as a rich farmer but he found
his servants cheated him so he went back to sleep. When he
eventually awoke again he wandered down the
mountainside to see what he could see.

He came upon a rock pool where a waterfall tumbled

down the rocks. A group of laughing girls were sitting dangling their toes in the water. The giant hid and watched. One of the girls was quieter than the others, but to the giant she was the prettiest. Her name was Elizabeth and she was to be married in a few days to the young duke. She and her friends chattered about the forthcoming celebrations as they paddled in the pool, and all the while the giant watched. When they skipped away, his heart grew sad. He realised just how very lonely he was.

He decided to try to win Elizabeth's heart. All through the night he worked. He covered the steep stone under the waterfall with white marble so it sparkled in the clear water. He lined the pool with silver, and filled it with darting golden fish. He covered the banks with rich green grass, planted with sweetly-smelling violets and forget-me-nots and deep blue hyacinths. Then he hid himself again.

When the girls arrived they were astonished, but Elizabeth looked thoughtful. She knew that some powerful enchantment had been at work. She wandered to the edge and looked deep into the silver pool, full of the golden fish.

345

And as she looked she heard a voice, whispering, whispering to her to step into the pool. There was a sudden splash, and as her friends looked round in alarm, Elizabeth slipped into the pool. The girls ran over to the pool and looked into the silver depths. In vain they tried to find her. When they went home and told the young duke, he came with all haste to the pool. All the giant's adornments had vanished. The waterfall fell over steep and black rocks, the silver lining and the golden fish had disappeared from the pool, and there was not a single flower to be seen. Sadly, the duke went back to the palace and nothing would cheer him.

Meanwhile Elizabeth found herself in the giant's garden. He begged her to stay with him and be his queen, but she told him she loved the duke and would not forsake him. The giant hoped she would forget the duke, but as the days passed he saw that she grew pale and sad. He wondered how he could cheer her, and change her mind. Then he remembered his magic staff. Whatever it touched would turn into any animal he wished for. He gave the staff to Elizabeth and for a few hours she was happy as, first a kitten then a dog then a canary appeared

347

thanks to the staff. But it was not long before she grew silent again.

Now the giant grew very good carrots, and he was very proud of his carrots. He pulled some for supper and Elizabeth said she had never tasted such delicious carrots in all her life, which was true. So the next day, the giant took Elizabeth out into the fields round the castle where the carrots grew. As far as the eye could see there were carrots, row upon row of them. Elizabeth asked the giant how many there were, but he couldn't tell her that at all. So she begged him to count at least one row, and as he began counting she quickly drew the staff out from under her cloak and touched a black stone that lay on the ground. It turned into a black horse with great hooves that pounded the earth as Elizabeth mounted its back and fled down the valley away, away from the giant.

The very next day, Elizabeth married her duke and

they lived happily ever after. The lonely giant went slowly back to his garden, and fell into a deep sleep. Many hundreds of years passed and still the giant never awoke. In time grass and plants and trees grew over the slumbering giant, and still he slept on. Over the years the mound that was the sleeping giant became known as Giant Mountain, and so it is still called today. So beware if you see great rows of carrots on a mountain side, you might be very near a sleeping giant!

The Mermaid of Zennor

a Cornish legend

The bell was ringing, calling the villagers of Zennor to Sunday service. It was a simple little granite towered church, built to withstand the wild winds and weather that could roll in from the sea. Matthew Trewella stood in the choir stalls and looked at the new bench he had been carving. It was nearly finished and wanted only one more panel to be carved.

As the voices of the congregation rang out in the hymns, a sweet pure voice was heard. A voice that no one had heard before. When the villagers turned to leave at the end of the service, there at the back of the little church stood the most beautiful woman any of them had ever seen. Her dress was made of soft rustling silk, at one moment green, the next blue, like the sea. Round her neck she wore a gleaming necklace of pearls, and her golden hair fell down her back almost to the floor.

As Matthew walked out, the woman placed her hand on his sleeve.

"Your carving is beautiful, Matthew."

Matthew blushed and turned his rough cap round and round in his great red hands, his deep blue eyes wary.

"Why, thank you ma'am," he managed to stutter before he fled out of the church. Where the beautiful lady went no one quite saw.

The next day Matthew was hard at work, carving the decoration of leaves that went round the edge of the bench when he heard the soft rustle of silk. There stood the woman again.

"What will you put in the last panel, Matthew?" she whispered. And she smiled into his deep blue eyes. Matthew sensed a strong smell of the sea in the tiny church as he bent to get up off his knees but when he looked up again, there was no sign of the woman.

The next Sunday the lady was in church again. She looked deep into Matthew's eyes as she sang the hymns, and when he walked slowly out, as if in a dream, she was waiting for him.

"Will you carve my image in the last panel, Matthew?" she asked and her voice was gentle and sighing like the withdrawing tide on a shingle beach. Matthew's deep blue eyes gazed far over her head, out towards the sea, but he did not reply. Only the schoolmaster and his wife noticed that the seat where the woman had sat was wet, wet with sea water. But they said nothing.

Time passed, and every Sunday the woman came to church. Matthew seemed like a man in a dream, his eyes always looking out to sea. The final panel was still not finished on the bench. November came, and with it the mist curled up from the sea. Night after night a light was to be seen late in the church. The gentle sound of wood chipping drifted out with the mist, but no one ventured into the church.

It was the parson who discovered the finished bench when he went in to open up the church one morning. The church floor was wet, wet with sea water. The stub of a candle stood among a great pile of wood shavings on the floor. The final panel of the bench was the best Matthew had ever carved. It was a mermaid, long hair falling down her back, the scales of her great fish tail in deep relief. She looked almost alive.

Matthew Trewella had not slept in his bed that night, nor was he ever seen again in Zennor. The mysterious woman never came to church again. The schoolmaster and his wife never talked of the wet seat. Only the fishermen would shake their heads as they sat talking on the winter's evenings. They would talk of the mermaid they had seen off the coast, and of the young man with the deep blue eyes who was always swimming by her side.

The Seven Ravens

a fairytale from Poland

There was once a poor widow who had seven great sons and a daughter. The daughter, Anne, was a good girl, but the seven brothers were wild as the hills. One day the widow was baking a blackberry pie. As she rolled out the pastry the whole noisy troop came shouting into the kitchen.

"Blackberry pie!" they yelled. "When will it be ready?"

"When it is cooked," she said crossly. "Let me finish then we can all eat." But the boys just ran about the hot kitchen, pushing and shoving each other and leaving great muddy bootmarks all over the clean floor.

"Oh, can't you be quiet! I wish, I wish you were ravens instead of great noisy boys," she cried. But then her eyes widened in horror as the boys shrank, and feathers covered their arms. Their mouths turned into beaks, and with seven deep croaks they flew out of the door. Anne rushed to the window, but the ravens were already out of sight. Together mother and daughter sat weeping, and not even the smell of burning pie could rouse them.

But the next day Anne said to her mother, "I am determined to find my brothers and bring them safely back home."

So she set off with nothing but her needle and thread and scissors in her pocket. She walked and walked and came across a curious little house in the woods. It was made of silver, and the woman who opened the door was dressed in a long silver robe. But she was not friendly.

"I am all behind today, and my husband will be home soon. There is no supper ready, and I have to mend his cloak," she said all in a rush.

"I could mend the cloak," said Anne taking out her needle, "and then you can cook the supper."

Well, the woman was delighted and opened the door wide. Anne sat quietly in the corner and with the tiniest stitches ever mended the beautiful cloak. When the husband, who was also dressed all in silver, came in he was very impressed with Anne's work, and invited her to join them for supper which was the most delicious roast chicken.

The silver man asked Anne where she was going so she told them the whole story of her brothers.

"Perhaps we can help you," said the silver man. "We are the moon's helpers and she sees most things on earth. I will ask her if she knows where your brothers are."

As the wife cleared the table after supper, she gave Anne the chicken bones.

"Keep these in your pocket, you never know when they might come in useful," and Anne did so.

When the silver man returned the next morning he told Anne that the moon had seen seven ravens flying round the Amber Mountain. When Anne asked him where the Amber Mountain was he told her to follow her nose until she could go no further. Anne thanked the silver couple and set off once again, her nose very firmly in front.

After several days she came to a halt. There in front of her was the Amber Mountain, its sides steep as glass. Anne did not know what to do, but then she remembered the chicken bones. She pushed one into the surface of the mountain and stood on it. Then she put the second bone in a little higher, and stood on that, and so she slowly, slowly climbed to the very top of the mountain. And there she found seven sad-looking ravens. They were her brothers!

But there was also an evil old witch sitting there too.

"Well, my dear, your brothers are under my spell, and the only way you can release them is by remaining silent for seven years. Not one single word or you will lose them for ever," and with an evil cackle she flew off.

Anne climbed down the mountain, and when she reached home her mother was delighted to see her. But Anne could tell her nothing. Four years passed in silence until one day Anne was out gathering firewood when a

royal hunting party came through the wood. The prince was very struck by Anne's quiet ways, but of course he couldn't get a word out of her. Thereafter he came by every day, and at length asked her to marry

him. She smiled her acceptance but never a word did she utter.

Three more years passed, and the prince and Anne had a baby son. Now the queen had never really approved of her son marrying such a poor girl, however pretty she might be, and she never lost an opportunity to make mischief. One day she rushed into the prince and accused Anne of trying to poison the baby. The prince was horrified but, of course, when he asked Anne if she had done such a terrible thing, she was unable to reply. So he sent her to the dungeons, and told her she had three days to explain herself or she would die.

The three days passed with Anne still not uttering a word. On the third day, she was brought out into the courtyard where everyone waited to see what would happen next.

Suddenly there was a great flapping of wings and

seven ravens landed in a circle around Anne. It was her brothers, and in a blink of an eye there they stood, restored to human shape. Well, you can imagine what a lot Anne had to tell! They all talked into the night. The queen had somehow gone missing, but no one seemed to mind too much. The seven brothers went to collect their mother, and when they all came back together the prince promised her that she would never have to do a day's work again!

The Twelve Windows

From 'Told Again' by Walter de la Mare

There was once a princess who lived alone with her father the king, the queen having died many years before. The princess was wise and gentle and loved her father very much, so much so that the king dreaded the day when the princess would marry and leave him alone in the empty palace. But she had promised she would never marry until she met a man who would have three chances to hide himself in the palace so cleverly that she could not see him. Now you might think this was not so difficult but the princess had witch's eyes and she could spy out the smallest thing like an ant or one tiny daisy on the palace lawn. She had a special room at the top of a tower in the palace which had twelve windows that the princess could look out of to practise her great skill.

Many princes and handsome young men came to court the princess but all failed to hide themselves well enough. Now there was a swineherd who would watch the princes and the handsome young men come and go, and after a while he thought he might just as well try himself to see if he could win the hand of the princess. When he arrived at the palace gate, the guards just laughed at him, but the watchman who was passing at

the time thought the young swineherd had an honest face.
So he lent him a cloak of green velvet, and the swineherd
was ushered into the princess's rooms.

Straightaway she saw that he had an honest face, but
she also saw his poor clothes under the cloak, and she saw
his heart beating against his ribs. She wished him luck, and
gave him an hour to hide. The swineherd went down,
down deep into the palace dungeons
and hid himself under a pile of
straw. When the hour was up,
the princess climbed up
into her special room

and looked through the first window. She could see no sign of the swineherd. She looked through the second window. She could see no sign of the swineherd. But then she looked through the third window, and there she could see him, lying under the straw. The princess was sorry as she realised that the young swineherd was the first of the many young men who had come to court her that she actually liked.

The next day, the swineherd went to the palace fish pond and, taking a deep breath, he plunged to the bottom of the pond and hid under the roots of the graceful water lilies. He waited and waited, his lungs bursting. The princess climbed up into her special room and

looked through the first window, then the second, the third, the fourth and the fifth. There was no sign of the swineherd, and the princess found she was pleased. She looked through the sixth and the seventh and the eighth. There was no sign of the swineherd and the princess found she was delighted. But then she looked through the ninth, and she saw the swineherd crouched in the pond, under the roots of the water lilies. The princess found she was full of sadness.

The young swineherd realised he was up against some powerful witchcraft, so that night he went to seek out his friend the white fox. He told her all about the princess and her witch's eyes, and he also told the fox that he had fallen in love with the princess. The fox just nodded and told him to get a good night's sleep. She woke him in the morning before it was light. When the swineherd was washed and dressed, the fox touched him with the tip of her tail, and he turned into a beautiful white mountain hare. Then she

turned herself into an old
woman and, taking the
hare in her arms, she
walked to the palace and
stood by the garden gate.

The princess was
walking in the palace
gardens, her face sad as she
thought of the swineherd who today faced his
last chance at becoming her husband. She saw an old
woman standing by the garden gate, with a white
mountain hare in her arms. The hare looked so beautiful
that the princess could not resist going up to stroke its fur.
The old woman who, of course, was really the clever fox,
gave the hare who, of course, was really the swineherd, to
the princess. The princess was amazed by the beauty of the
hare and by the softness of its fur, but when she went to

give it back, the old woman had disappeared. The princess placed the hare on her shoulder and together they climbed the stairs to the room with the twelve windows.

The hare crept round under the princess's hair as she looked out of the first window. There was no sign of the swineherd. She looked out of all the windows until she came to the twelfth. There was no sign of the swineherd. With a beating heart she went to look out of the last window. She so wanted not to see the swineherd. She looked and looked again. She could not see him! The one thing witch's eyes cannot do is see behind them, and so the swineherd had won the hand of the princess. The hare darted down the stairs while the princess was still crying with delight, and ran out of the palace to where the fox was waiting. She touched the hare with the tip of her tail and there stood the swineherd once again.

He thanked the fox profusely and than ran back to

the palace as fast as ever he could. There he found the princess standing in the garden looking everywhere for him. They went to see the king, and the whole story came out. The princess and the swineherd said they loved each other. The swineherd said he did not want to live anywhere else in the land. So the king did not lose his daughter. The princess married a man she really liked. The swineherd gained everything from just having a try. The white fox was invited to the wedding, and they all lived happily ever after.

Rapunzel

a retelling from the original fairytale by the Brothers Grimm

O nce upon a time there lived a man and his wife who for years and years had wanted a child. One day the wife was looking sadly out of the window. Winter was coming but in the next door garden, which was surrounded by a huge great wall, she could just see rows and rows of delicious vegetables. In particular, she could see a huge bunch of rapunzel, a special kind of lettuce. Her mouth watered, it looked so fresh and green.

"Husband, I shall not rest until I have some of that rapunzel growing next door," she whispered.

The husband clambered over the wall and quickly picked a small bunch which he took back to his wife. She made it into a salad, and ate it all up. But the next day, all she could think of was how delicious it had been so she asked him to pick her some more.

He clambered over the wall, and was picking a small bunch of the rapunzel when a voice behind him hissed, "So you are the one who has been stealing my rapunzel!"

When he spun round, there stood a witch and she looked very angry indeed. The husband was terrified, but he tried to explain that his wife had been desperate for some fresh leaves for her salad.

"You may take all the leaves you require then, but you must give me your first child when she is born," smiled the witch, and it was not a nice smile. The husband was greatly relieved, however, for he knew that there was little chance of his wife ever having a daughter so he fled back over the wall, clutching the bunch of rapunzel. He did not tell his wife of his meeting with the witch for he thought it would only frighten her, and he soon forgot all about his adventure.

But it all came back to him when nine months later his wife gave birth to a beautiful baby girl. No sooner had she laid the baby in her cradle, than the witch appeared to claim the child. The wife wept, the husband pleaded but nothing could persuade the witch to forget the husband's awful promise, and so she took the tiny baby away.

The witch called the baby Rapunzel.
She grew into a beautiful girl with long,
long hair as fine as spun gold. When
she was sixteen, the witch took
Rapunzel and locked her into a
tall tower so no one would see
how beautiful she was. The witch
threw away the key to the tower, and so
whenever she wanted to visit Rapunzel
she would call out, "Rapunzel, Rapunzel,
let down your hair," and Rapunzel would
throw her golden plait of hair out of the window
at the top of the tower so the witch could slowly
scramble up.

Now one day it happened that a handsome young
prince was riding through the woods. He heard the witch
call out to Rapunzel and he watched her climb up the

tower. After the witch had gone, the prince came to the
bottom of the tower and he called up, "Rapunzel,
Rapunzel, let down your hair," and he climbed quickly
up the shining golden plait. You can imagine
Rapunzel's astonishment when she saw the
handsome Prince standing in front of her but
she was soon laughing at his stories. When
he left, he promised to come again

the next day, and he did. And the next, and the next, and soon they had fallen in love with each other.

One day as the witch clambered up Rapunzel exclaimed, "You are slow! The prince doesn't take nearly as long to climb up the tower," but no sooner were the words out of her mouth than she realised her terrible mistake. The witch seized the long, long golden plait and cut it off. She drove Rapunzel far, far away from the tower, and then sat down to await the prince. When the witch heard him calling, she threw the golden plait out of the window. Imagine the prince's dismay when he sprang into the room only to discover the horrible witch instead of his beautiful Rapunzel! When the witch told him he would never see his Rapunzel again, in his grief he flung himself out of the tower. He fell into some brambles which scratched his eyes so he could no longer see.

And thus he wandered the land, always asking if

anyone had seen his Rapunzel. After seven long years, he came to the place where she had hidden herself away. As he stumbled down the road, Rapunzel recognised him and with a great cry of joy she ran up to him and took him gently by the hand to her little cottage in the woods. As she washed his face, two of her tears fell on the prince's eyes and his sight came back. And so they went back to his palace and lived happily ever after. The witch, you will be pleased to hear, had not been able to get down from the tower, so she did NOT live happily ever after!

Teeny-Tiny

an English folk tale

Once upon a time there lived a teeny-tiny old woman. She lived in a teeny-tiny house in a teeny-tiny street with a teeny-tiny cat. One day the teeny-tiny woman decided to go out for a teeny-tiny walk. She put on her teeny-tiny boots and her teeny-tiny bonnet, and off she set.

When she had walked a teeny-tiny way down the teeny-tiny street, she went through a teeny-tiny gate into a teeny-tiny graveyard, which was a teeny-tiny shortcut to the teeny-tiny meadow. Well, she had only taken a few teeny-tiny steps when she saw a teeny-tiny bone lying on top of a teeny-tiny grave. She thought that would do very well to make some teeny-tiny soup for supper so she put the teeny-tiny bone in her teeny-tiny pocket and went home at once to her teeny-tiny house.

Now the teeny-tiny woman was tired when she reached her teeny-tiny house so she did not make the teeny-tiny soup immediately but put the teeny-tiny bone into her teeny-tiny cupboard. Then she sat in her teeny-tiny chair and put her teeny-tiny feet up and had a teeny-tiny sleep. But she had only been asleep a teeny-tiny time when she woke up at the sound of a teeny-tiny voice coming from her teeny-tiny cupboard. The teeny-tiny voice said, "Where is my teeny-tiny bone?"

Well, the teeny-tiny woman was a teeny-tiny bit frightened so she wrapped her teeny-tiny shawl round her teeny-tiny head and went to sleep again. She had only been asleep a teeny-tiny time when the teeny-tiny voice came from the teeny-tiny cupboard again, a teeny-tiny bit louder this time. "Where is my teeny-tiny bone?"

The teeny-tiny woman was a teeny-tiny bit more frightened than last time so she hid under the teeny-tiny cushions, but she could not go back to sleep, not even a teeny-tiny bit. Then the teeny-tiny voice came again and this time it was even a teeny-tiny bit louder. "Where is my teeny-tiny bone?"

This time the teeny-tiny woman sat up in her teeny-tiny chair and said in her loudest teeny-tiny voice, "TAKE IT!"

There was a teeny-tiny silence, and then a teeny-tiny ghost ran out of the teeny-tiny house, down the teeny-tiny street, through the teeny-tiny gate into the teeny-tiny graveyard – with the teeny-tiny bone clutched very tightly in its teeny-tiny hand! And the teeny-tiny woman never took even a teeny-tiny walk there ever again!

Baba Yaga, The Bony-Legged

a Russian folk tale

There was once a wicked woman who hated her stepdaughter so much that she pushed the little girl out of doors and told her to go and borrow a needle and thread from Baba Yaga, the bony-legged witch. The girl's stepmother did it when her husband was out at work, so the little girl had no one to turn to and she was terrified. Baba Yaga had iron teeth, and lived in the middle of the deep, dark forest, in a hut which moved about on hens' legs. Neverthless, the girl dared not disobey her cruel stepmother. So off she went into the deep, dark forest.

The little girl was soon among tall, prickly trees that whispered all around her, and she quite forgot which way was which. Big tears began to glisten in her eyes.

"Do not weep, little girl," came a cheerful voice. The little girl looked up to see that a little nightingale was talking to her. "You are a kind-hearted girl and I will tell you what I can to help you. Pick up things that you come across along the path and make sure you use them wisely."

So the little girl set off again, further into the deep, dark forest. As she walked along, she saw a neatly folded handkerchief lying among the pine-needles, and she put it in her pocket. A little further on, she took some ribbons that were dangling from the branches. A few steps on, she picked up a little can of oil that lay amongst some rocks. Next, she came across a big, juicy bone and then a large maple-leaf sprinkled with some tasty-looking morsels of meat – and then her pocket was full.

It wasn't long
before some big iron
gates came into view up ahead,
and beyond them was Baba Yaga's hut, running about on
its hens' legs. The little girl shivered with fear. Suddenly a
howling wind rose up which sent the branches of the trees
whipping fiercely around her head. I'll never get near that
horrible hut at this rate, the little girl realised, ducking the
boughs coming at her thick and fast. She thought quickly.
She pulled out the ribbons and tied them onto the trees,
and as soon as she did so, the wind dropped to a gentle
breeze and the branches became still.

Then the little girl tried to push open the gates, but a dreadful creaking and groaning tore the air. The girl took the oil can from her pocket and gave the hinges a good oiling. After that, the gate opened without a squeak, and the girl passed through.

All of a sudden, a drooling, snarling dog came running at her out of nowhere, barking fit to wake the dead. Quick as a flash, the girl grabbed the big, juicy bone and threw it to the dog. He forgot his attack immediately and lay down and began to gnaw.

Now the girl faced the hut itself, scuttling about on its awful scaly legs. And there on the steps stood BABA YAGA THE BONY-LEGGED!

"Come in, my dear!" grinned the witch, showing her iron teeth. "While I'm searching for that needle and thread you want, you can have a nice bath and do my spinning for me."

Baba Yaga gripped the girl's arm with her claw-like fingers and pulled her up the steps into the house. "Run her a bath and be quick about it!" she screamed at her pale-faced maid, before whispering "Make sure you scrub her well, all ready for eating." Then Baba Yaga the bony-legged bustled away.

The pale-faced maid began to hurry about filling the bath with water, and the little girl saw that she was trembling with fear of Baba Yaga the bony-legged. "I am sorry for you having to live and work here," the little girl said. "Here, have this handkerchief as a little present to cheer you up."

"Oh thank you," the pale-faced maid sighed, gazing in delight at the lovely embroidery. "I will use a teacup instead of a jug to fill the bath, so you have more time to escape."

Then the little girl noticed a skinny black cat in the

corner. "You don't look as if you've eaten properly for ages," she said, stroking his tatty fur. "Here, have these scraps of meat."

"Oh thank you," the skinny black cat purred, neatly washing his paws. "I will do the spinning for you, so you have more time to escape. Now take this magic towel and comb and run for your life. When you hear Baba Yaga coming, throw each of them behind you, one by one."

So the little girl took the magic towel and comb and began to run for her life through the deep, dark forest, while the cat sat down at the spinning wheel, tangled the wool into a big mess and hid behind it, and began to spin.

Several times, the witch passed the open door of the room and peered in. But when she heard the whirr of the spinning wheel and saw the pile of tangled wool, she went away content that the little girl was working hard. But by and by, the witch began to get suspicious that the pile of wool wasn't getting any smaller. "Are you sure you know how to spin properly, little girl?" she screeched.

"Yes, thank you," yowled the cat, trying to sound like the little girl but failing terribly. Then Baba Yaga the bony-legged screamed with fury. She rushed into the room and grabbed the cat by the scruff of the neck. "Why did you let the girl escape?" she howled.

"You've never given me anything to eat but leftovers," the cat hissed. "That kind-hearted girl gave me tasty morsels of meat."

Then Baba Yaga stalked over to the pale-faced maid and slapped her. "Why did you let her escape?" she howled.

"You've never given me a single present," the pale-faced maid shouted. "That kind-hearted girl gave me a lovely hanky."

Then Baba Yaga stormed outside and threw a stick at the dog.

"Why did you let the girl escape?" she howled.

"You've never given me a bone," the dog barked. "That kind-hearted girl gave me a big, juicy one to chew on."

Then Baba Yaga kicked the iron gates. "Why did you let the girl escape?" she howled.

"You've let us get all stiff and rusty," they creaked. "That kind-hearted girl soothed our aching joints with lots of lovely oil."

Finally, Baba Yaga punched the birch trees. "Why did you let the girl escape?" she howled.

"You've never once decorated our branches," they roared, "but that kind-hearted girl tied beautiful ribbons all over us."

Then Baba Yaga gnashed her iron teeth and jumped on her broomstick and raced off through the deep, dark forest after the little girl. The little girl heard the swish of the air and knew she was coming and threw down the magic towel. Suddenly a wide rushing river appeared before Baba Yaga, splashing all over her broomstick and soaking it so badly that it could no longer fly. Spitting and cursing, Baba Yaga had to get off and slowly wade across. Then Baba Yaga was off and running . . .

The little girl heard the pounding of Baba Yaga's footsteps and knew she was coming, and she threw down the magic comb. All at once, a jungle sprang up in front of Baba Yaga, so thick and dense and tangled that Baba Yaga the bony-legged could do nothing to find her way through. She squawked and gnashed her iron teeth, and stormed back to her horrible hut, shouting all the way.

The little girl saw her father standing at the door of their house, and she rushed to tell him all about her stepmother's evil plot. Her father pushed the wicked woman out of doors and drove her into the magic jungle – after which, she was never seen again. Then the little girl and her father lived happily on their own, and the nightingale came to visit every day.

The Selfish Giant

retold from the original tale by Oscar Wilde

Once there was a beautiful garden in which the children used to play every day on their way home from school. The children didn't think that the beautiful garden belonged to anyone in particular. But one day a huge giant strode in and boomed, "What are you all doing here? This is MY garden. Get lost!" Seven years ago, the giant had gone to visit his friend the Cornish ogre. Now he was back and he wanted his garden all to himself.

Of course, the children ran away at once. But the giant wasn't satisfied. Straight away, he put up a high fence all the way around his garden with a noticeboard outside which read: TRESPASSERS WILL BE PROSECUTED. He really was a very selfish giant.

Now the poor children had nowhere to play. But the giant didn't give any thought to that. He was too busy wondering why the blossom had fallen from the trees, why the flowers had withered, and why all the birds seemed to have flown away. Surely it is meant to be the springtime, the giant thought to himself as he looked out of the window and saw huge flakes of snow beginning to tumble from the sky. Frost painted the trees silver. A blanket of ice chilled the ground and hardened the plants into stiff, lifeless spikes. Day after day, the north wind roared around the giant's garden, zooming around his roof and howling down his chimney pots. And the hail came to, battering on the giant's windows until he bellowed with annoyance and clapped his hands over his ears against the noisy rattling.

Then one Saturday, the giant woke up to hear a sound he had almost forgotten – it was a bird, chirruping and cheeping in his garden. A beautiful perfume tickled the giant's nose . . . It was the scent of flowers! "Spring has come at last!" the giant beamed, and he pulled on his clothes and ran outside into his garden.

The giant couldn't believe what he saw. The snow had melted, the frost and ice were gone, the sky was blue and the breeze was gentle and warm. And there were children everywhere. They had crept back into his garden through a hole that had worn away in the fence. Now children were sitting in trees heavy with ripe fruit. Playing among flowerbeds filled with nodding blossoms. Running over emerald green grass scattered with daisies and buttercups. And the sound of their happy laughter filled the air.

Only in one corner of the garden was it

still winter. A little boy was standing in a patch of snow, looking up at the bare branches of a chestnut tree and crying because he couldn't reach it. The giant's heart ached as he watched. "Now I know what makes my garden beautiful," the giant murmured. "It is the children. How selfish I have been!"

The giant strode through the garden towards the sobbing little boy. The giant scooped him up gently and set him among the icy boughs of the chestnut tree.

At once, broad green leaves appeared all over the

branches and down below, the snow vanished and it was spring. The little boy's face brightened into a huge smile and he reached his arms up around the giant's neck and hugged him.

"It is your garden now, little children," laughed the giant, and the children skipped about delightedly. The giant took his axe and knocked down the fence and had more fun than he had ever had in his life by playing with them all day. Only one thing spoiled the giant's new

happiness. He looked all over his garden for the little boy whom he had helped into the tree, but he was nowhere to be found. The giant loved the little boy the best, because he had kissed him, and he longed more than anything to see his friend again.

Many years passed by and the children came every day to play in the beautiful garden. The giant became old and creaky and eventually he could no longer run about and let the children climb over him as he had done. The giant sat in a special armchair so he could watch the children enjoying themselves. "My garden is very beautiful," he would say to himself, 'but the children are the most beautiful things of all." Sometimes the giant's huge grey head would nod forwards and he would begin to snore, and the children would creep away quietly so they didn't disturb him. And one afternoon, the giant woke from such a little doze to see an astonishing sight.

In the farthest corner of his garden was a golden tree he had never seen before. The giant's heart leaped for joy, for standing underneath it was the boy he had loved.

The giant heaved himself up from his armchair and shuffled across the grass as fast as his old legs would take him. But when he drew near the little boy, his face grew black as thunder. There were wounds on the little boy's palms and on his feet. "Who has dared to hurt you?" boomed the giant. "Tell me, and I will go after them with my big axe!"

"These are the marks of love," the little boy smiled, and he took the giant's hand. "Once, you let me play in your garden," the little boy said. "And today, you shall come with me to mine, which is in Paradise."

And when the children came running to play that afternoon, they found the giant lying dead under the beautiful tree, covered with a beautiful blanket of snowy-white blossoms.

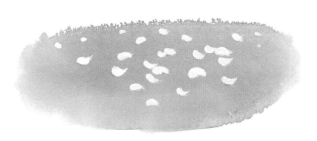

In the Castle of Giant Cruelty

retold from an original tale in John Bunyan's The Pilgrim's Progress

There was once a dark, ugly city where no one seemed to be happy. But none of the grumpy, scowling citizens ever thought of leaving because they knew nothing of life outside the city walls. Huge, flat plains of mud surrounded the city as far as the eye could see. No one had ever braved the danger of trying to wade through them, so no one even knew if there was anything beyond the swamps. There were rumours of a distant city where the sun always shone and where the people lived happily together – but no one really believed it existed . . . that is, except for a man called Christian.

For a long time, Christian had been growing more and more miserable with his life in the grim, depressing city. But it was the strange, glowing light that finally made him decide to leave. It was some weeks ago that Christian had first glimpsed the light, far away in the distance, beyond the mud flats. No one else seemed to be able to see it. They just shuffled around with their hands in their pockets, looking at the pavements as usual. But Christian thought the light was beautiful. "I shall leave this dreadful city and somehow reach the place the light is coming from," he decided. "Or I shall die in the attempt," he added.

Christian didn't take anything with him. He just got up the next morning and instead of making his usual way to work, he walked towards the gates that led out of the city. As people realised that Christian meant to leave town, they began to laugh and jeer at him. "You must be mad!" they mocked. "You'll be floundering in that mud by nightfall and no one will come to rescue you!" But Christian didn't listen to them. He just heaved open the rusty, creaky city gates and strode out into the swamps.

As soon as Christian was outside the city, he felt as if he had left his cares and troubles behind him. Determinedly, he began walking towards the light in the distance. He walked . . . and walked . . . and walked . . .

until he had left the city so far behind that he couldn't see its dark, smoky outline any more. He walked and walked until he dropped with thirst and hunger and exhaustion.

Christian didn't have the strength to lift himself back up. He closed his eyes and everything went black.

It was having a huge bucket of water sloshed over his face that finally brought Christian back to his senses. He sat bolt upright, gasping and choking and spluttering out the iciness that filled his nose and mouth.

"I am the Giant Cruelty!" boomed the loudest voice that Christian had ever heard. He looked up and began to tremble. He was in a stone room the size of a cave, and standing over him was a man as tall as his house back in the city. The giant had blood-shot eyes and blackened teeth and long, claw-like nails. "What were you doing, trespassing on my land?" Giant Cruelty thundered.

"I'm v-v-very s-s-s-orry," Christian stuttered. "I d-d-didn't realise I was trespassing."

"That is a pitiful excuse!" the giant bellowed. "Now you are no longer a trespasser. You are a prisoner.."

The giant's eyes lit up with amusement and he cackled evilly. "I shall enjoy watching you rot in my dungeons!" he boomed, and scooped Christian up in his mighty fist.

Christian's heart thumped as he felt himself being carried down a long flight of steps. He shivered at the echoing of the giant's footsteps all around and at the damp chill in the air. He wrinkled his nose in disgust as a vile stench filled his nostrils.

Suddenly, the giant's fist opened and Christian was thrown onto the stone floor of a dungeon. A rat scampered up and squeaked in his face, and Christian sprang to his feet with shock.

"Have this bread and water," Giant Cruelty ordered, hurling a mouldy loaf at Christian and slamming down a bucket of foul-smelling water.

"You have to stay alive so I can come back tomorrow and watch you scream and cry and beg for mercy." Giant Cruelty chuckled. He slammed the door of the dungeon, locked it with a massive iron key, and stomped back up the stairs.

Christian swallowed hard and turned away from the locked door. He wasn't the only prisoner after all. Six faces peered out from the shadows – faces that looked even more hungry and thirsty and despairing than his own.

"How long have you been here?" Christian gulped.

"So long that we have forgotten our own names," one man sighed.

"The giant only feeds us once a week," a woman whimpered, eyeing Christian's bread and water.

"Here," Christian decided at once. "Come and join in my share with me. If we all stay strong and help each other, maybe we can find a way out of here together."

The desperate men and women didn't need inviting twice. They crept out of the shadows and fell on the loaf ravenously.

At that very moment, a spine-tingling CREAK! filled the air and the dungeon door swung wide open. To Christian's astonishment, a golden key had appeared in the lock. There were words down the shaft which read: the Key of Kindness.

Christian didn't stop to wonder at the strange key. He just grabbed it and urged, "Come on everybody!", and hurried everyone out of the dungeon and up the stairs. The Key of Kindness somehow fitted every locked door they came to and the giant seemed to have disappeared altogether.

Christian and his new friends didn't stop running

until they had left the castle far behind them. Then they hugged each other, panting, and turned towards the glowing light. Christian smiled. Now he could see the faint outline of a golden city – and it was much, much closer than before. As he set off on his journey once more, he felt a new feeling in his heart. It was hope.

David and the Giant

a tale from the Old Testament of the Bible

How David wished he could be just like his three older brothers! They were away fighting in the war with the fierce Philistines. But David was too young to join the great army of King Saul, like them. He was too young to strap on his armour and gird on his sword and face the pagan warriors, like they had. He was too young to fight to defend his country and his religion, to fight for his God, like they were.

Well, that's what David's father, the white-haired Jesse, kept telling him, anyway. So David found himself stuck at home looking after his father's sheep and listening to his father worry day and night about his other sons away at the battlefront.

One evening, David returned home from his peaceful day out on the pastures to find that his father was packing some grain, bread and cheeses. "I'm sending you to take these supplies to your brothers, David," said old Jesse, with an anxious look on his face. "It will be a dangerous trip, and I'm in half a mind not to send you at all. But they can't have very much to keep them going – and besides, I'm desperate to hear news of how they are."

David's heart leapt within his chest. At last, he was going on an adventure! He tried not to look too excited to be leaving his old father all alone at home, but he couldn't help the bright glint in his eye as he waved goodbye and set off on his horse.

After several days of hard riding, David had gained a bruised bottom and an aching back, and had lost a little of his reckless enthusiasm. In fact, when David finally reached King Saul's army camp, he no longer felt very excited at all. He found the soldiers exhausted and running away from the battlefield as fast as their wobbly legs would carry them. The retreating troops threatened to trample David underfoot as they swarmed back into the camp, and David was very glad when he finally recognised the familiar faces of his brothers among the retreating troops. "Whatever is going on?" David gasped.

"It's a giant – a real, live giant!" one of his brothers panted. "Whenever we go out to face the Philistine army in a battle, their troops don't come out to meet us. Instead, they send the giant Goliath, who challenges us to settle things by a duel – just him against one of us. It sounds fair enough – but you ought to see the size of him! There's no way any one in their right mind would face him alone! So we run away and Goliath and the Philistines stand there hurling insults at us."

At that, little David felt his blood begin to boil. You mean to say that no one has tried to beat this giant? he marvelled. Our whole army is a laughing stock? And he marched off to find King Saul. At first, King Saul was highly amused when his guards showed a little shepherd boy into his tent, who demanded, "I want you to let me fight Goliath! God has given me the strength to fight lions and bears when I'm looking after my sheep, and now he'll give me the strength to fight the giant, too!" There was a strange light of faith gleaming in the boy's eyes, so, much against his better judgement, King Saul decided to let the little shepherd boy have a go after all.

The king brought his own, very best, armour for David and helped dress him up in it. But the armour

totally swamped him and he could hardly move in it. So
David took the whole caboodle
off again. There he stood in his
simple shepherd's robe with his
crook, his catapult and a bag
of five round stones. And that's
how he strode out to face the
giant . . .

Goliath was far and
away the biggest man that
David had ever seen. He had
legs like tree trunks and carried
a spear the size of a battering
ram. When the giant saw the
tiny figure of the little shepherd
boy coming out to meet him, he
threw back his head and

roared with laughter. Then he stomped forwards over the earth, ready to rip David apart like a rag doll.

David gulped as the mighty man came storming towards him. He could feel the ground shaking as the giant thundered nearer, and he set a stone onto his catapult. Now he could see the big scar on the giant's chin and the way his bristly eyebrows joined in the middle. David took aim and fired – WHAM! the little stone sank right into the centre of the giant's forehead.

"What happened?" Goliath gasped, as he collapsed.

He never found out, because David rushed up, drew the giant's own sword and hacked off the wicked giant's head. And King Saul's army chased the stunned Philistine soldiers all the way back to their own cities.

The Fisherman and the Bottle

a tale from The Arabian Nights

The fisherman was having a very bad day. The first time he had cast his nets in to the Arabian Sea, all he had pulled out was an old boot. The second time, all he had pulled out was a broken pot full of mud. The third time he had cast his nets, and all he had pulled in was an old copper bottle. But there was something about the bottle that stopped the fisherman from hurling it back into the deeps. Perhaps it was the way the stopper glinted in the light. Or maybe it was the strange wax seal around the neck, highly decorated with strange markings. It might even have been the fact that the

413

fisherman
could have sworn he
heard a faint noise coming
from inside. In any case, something
made the fisherman plunge his hand into
his pocket for his penknife, slash the
wax seal around the neck, and draw
out the heavy stopper.

The fisherman turned the copper
bottle upside down and shook it.

All that came out was a trickle of dust as fine as sand . . . a trickle of dust that seemed to blow upwards with the wind, instead of falling down . . . a trickle of dust that became a wisp of smoke . . . a wisp of smoke that became a puff of mist . . . a puff of mist that became a cloud billowing overhead . . . a cloud that formed huge feet and legs, and an enormous body, and strong arms and hands – and a massive, fierce, bald head with golden earrings and a long moustache and cruel eyes. In other words, there was a gigantic genie towering over him.

"Kneel before me, you spawn of a quivering jellyfish!" the genie roared. "Prepare to meet your death!"

"What have I done?" the terrified fisherman begged, falling to the sand. "I know the story of Aladdin and the genie of the lamp. Haven't I set you free? Aren't you meant to grant me wishes?"

"You have indeed set me free," the gigantic genie bellowed, "but it is FAR TOO LATE for wishes! For the first hundred years that I was trapped inside that copper prison, I did indeed swear that I would grant three wishes to anyone who set me free – no matter how greedy they were. But no one helped me, and I grew impatient. For the next two hundred years, I swore that I would give never-ending riches to anyone who set me free. But no one helped me, and I grew angry. For the next five hundred years, I swore that I would give an entire kingdom to anyone who set me free. But no one helped me – and I grew furious. It was then that I swore that the very next person I saw would taste my revenge. Now I have been trapped inside that copper prison for TWO THOUSAND YEARS. And it is you who will have the honour of receiving my punishment!"

The fisherman shuddered as the genie drew an

enormous, shining, curved sword from his belt. He began to think fast if there were some way he could save himself . . .

To the genie's astonishment, the fisherman gave a friendly wink. "Come on now," the fisherman smirked, "enough of this fooling around. The way you appeared from nowhere like that was really very impressive, but I should tell you that I simply don't believe in magic."

"What do you mean, you don't believe in magic?" the genie roared, his face as black as soot.

"Well, sorcerers and genies and spells – no one believes in all that old rubbish nowadays," sniggered the fisherman, scornfully.

"Old rubbish!" blustered the genie, quite lost for words.

"So we've both had a bit of a laugh and a joke, haven't we?" continued the fisherman, quite calmly. "Now, you just tell me where you hid to make it look like you came out of the bottle, and I'll congratulate you on your fantastic trick. Then you can tell me where you're going to perform your conjuring show next time and I'll promise to bring lots of gullible friends who'll pay good money to watch you. And then we'll both shake hands on it and go home to our wives. What do you say?"

"How dare you call me a fake!" boomed the raging genie, as green smoke hissed out of his ears. "I'll show you that I'm real! I'll show you that I'm the most terrifying genie that ever came out of a bottle – I'll prove it to you, by getting back into it right now!"

Suddenly the genie's massive face began to melt, his arms and legs began to blur, his huge body began to shimmer in the air. His features became formless and shifting like a great cloud of mist. Then the cloud narrowed into a spiral of smoke that funnelled round and down and round and down . . . and right into the neck of the bottle.

As the very last wisp disappeared inside, the fisherman grabbed the heavy stopper and rammed it into the neck of the bottle as hard as he could.

"I shall never cast another net as long as I live," gasped the sweating fisherman, and he hurled the bottle as far as he could out into the ocean.

So if you're ever at the beach and you see a copper bottle bobbing about in the water or washed up on the shore, be very careful before you open it, won't you . . .

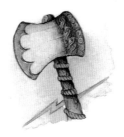

The Thunder God Gets Married

a Norse legend

U p in heaven, Thor the thunder god was furious. Someone had stolen his magic hammer. Thor's magic hammer was the terror of the gods. Whenever he threw it, it killed anything that it touched and it always returned to his hand. It was perhaps the most deadly weapon that the gods possessed to protect them against their enemies, the giants.

Now the raging Thor's roaring sounded like the clouds were clashing together. His face was so black with anger that it sent a dark shadow over the whole sky. As Thor grabbed blazing lightning bolts and hurled them through the clouds, the mischief-maker god, Loki, came nervously to see him. "I have good news, my angry friend," Loki explained. "I have used my cunning to find out that it is the giant Thrym who has stolen your hammer. He has agreed to give it back on one condition – that he has the most beautiful of all the goddesses, Freya, as his bride."

The thunder god's sulky face brightened a little and he charged off to find Freya straight away. "Put on your best dress, Freya!" Thor boomed, throwing open her wardrobe doors. "You have to marry the giant Thrym so I can get my magic hammer back."

Freya's eyes flickered with cold fire. "Excuse me, Thor," she said, calmly. "Would you care to repeat that?"

"You-have-to-marry-the-giant-Thrym-so-I-can-get-my-magic-hammer-back!" the impatient thunder god cried at top speed.

Freya stood glaring, her hands on her hips. "Firstly

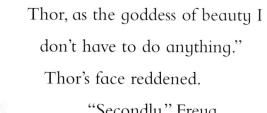

Thor, as the goddess of beauty I
don't have to do anything."
Thor's face reddened.

"Secondly," Freya
continued, "I wouldn't
marry that ugly monster
Thrym if he were the only
creature left in the world."

The ashamed thunder god hung his head.

"Thirdly," Freya finished, "it's your problem, you
sort it out."

"Sorry, Freya," Thor mumbled, shuffling about a bit.
Then he turned and stormed back to Loki. The two gods
sat down glumly and wracked their brains to come up
with another way to get back the hammer.

"How about . . ." Thor started to suggest. Then he
shook his head. "No, no good."

"What if . . ." Loki began. Then his face fell. "No, it would never work."

It looked as if Thor's magic hammer would have to stay in the land of the giants forever – until the god Heimdall had an idea.

"That's absolutely out of the question!" Thor thundered.

"Outrageous!" Loki squealed. "I'll never do it!"

"Well, you come up with another plan then," Heimdall laughed, knowing that there wasn't one.

That night, the giant Thrym was delighted to see a chariot with a bride and bridesmaid in it rumbling up to his castle. "It's Freya!" the gormless giant gasped with delight. "I shall gladly give back Thor's magic hammer in return for the most beautiful wife in the world!" The overjoyed giant commanded a magnificent banquet to be prepared and his guests to be sent for at once.

But Thrym wouldn't have been so overjoyed if he could have seen what was underneath the veils of his bride and bridesmaid – the angry, highly-embarrassed faces of Thor and Loki! As it was, the giant was far too excited to notice how big and clumsy the bride and bridesmaid looked in their frilly dresses. Thrym didn't take in that the women had low, gruff voices and huge, hairy hands. And he hardly thought twice about the way that Freya swigged down two whole barrels of beer and ate an entire roast ox.

When all the guests had eaten and drunk their fill, the beaming Thrym got to his feet to make a speech. "My wife and I," he began, blushing bright red, "would like to thank you all for coming here today to celebrate this happy occasion with us. Freya has made me the luckiest being in the whole universe. And now, I will keep my word and give back the magic hammer I stole from that ugly thug of a thunder god."

There was a roll of drums as one of Thrym's servants brought in the magic hammer on a cushion. Thrym held it high in the air for his marvelling guests to admire, then with a grand flourish, he presented it to his bride.

"The ugly thug of a thunder god thanks you!" roared Thor, ripping off his veil and springing to his feet. And before Thrym and his guests could really take in the trick, they were lying dead on the floor and the wedding feast was unexpectedly over.

All the gods were truly relieved to have the magic hammer back in Thor's hands in heaven, where it belonged. But it was a long time before Thor and Loki could laugh with the other gods about how charming they both looked in a dress!

Favourites

Hansel and Gretel

a retelling from the original tale by the Brothers Grimm

At the edge of a deep, dark forest there lived a poor woodcutter and his wife, a mean spiteful woman, and their two children Hansel and Gretel. The family was very poor and there was often very little food on the table.

One dreadful day there was no food at all and everyone went to bed hungry. Hansel could not sleep, and so it was that he heard his mother talking to his father. "Husband," she said in her thin spiteful voice, "there are too many mouths to feed. You must leave the children in the forest tomorrow."

"Wife, I cannot abandon our children, there are wolves in the forest!" said the poor woodcutter.

But his wife would give him no peace until he had agreed to her wicked plan. Hansel felt his heart grow icy cold. But he was a clever boy and so he slipped out of the house and filled his pockets with the shiny white stones that lay scattered around the house.

The next morning they all rose early and Hansel and Gretel followed their father deep into the forest. He lit them a fire and told them he was going to gather wood and would be back to collect them. He left them, tears falling down his face.

The day passed slowly. Hansel kept their fire going but when night fell, it grew very cold and they could hear all kinds of rustling under the shadowy trees. Gretel could not understand why their father had not come back to collect them, so Hansel had to tell her that their mother

had told the woodcutter to leave them there deliberately.

"But don't worry, Gretel," he said with a smile, "I will lead us back home," and there, clear in the moonlight, he showed her the line of shiny white stones that he had dropped from his pocket one by one that morning as their father had led them into the forest. They were soon home where there father greeted them with great joy. But their mother was not pleased.

Some time passed. They managed to survive with very

little to eat but another day came when Hansel heard his mother demanding that the woodcutter leave them in the forest again. This time when Hansel went to collect some more shiny pebbles, he found his mother had locked the door and he couldn't get out.

In the morning, their father gave them each a small piece of bread, and then led them even deeper into the forest than before. All day long, Hansel comforted Gretel and told her that this time he had left a trail of breadcrumbs to lead them safely back home. But when the moon rose and the children set off there was not a breadcrumb to be seen. The birds had eaten every last one. There was nothing to do but go to sleep under one of the great big trees and wait to see what they might do in the morning.

All next day they walked and walked, but they saw nothing but more and more great trees. And the next day was the same. By this time they were not only cold and very hungry but deeply frightened. It looked as if they would never ever be able to find a way out of the forest.But then just as it was getting dark, they came to a little clearing and there stood the most extraordinary house.

The walls were made of gingerbread, the windows of fine spun sugar and the tiles on the roof were brightly striped sweets. Hansel and Gretel could not believe their good luck and they were soon breaking off little bits of the amazing house to eat. But then a little voice came from inside.

"Nibble, nibble, little mouse,

Who is that eating my sweet house?"

Out of the front door came a very old woman. She smiled very sweetly at the children and said, "Dear children, you don't need to eat my house. Come inside and I will give you plenty to eat and you shall sleep in warm cosy beds tonight." Hansel and Gretel needed no second asking. They were soon tucked up, warm and full of hot milk and ginger biscuits and apples. They both fell asleep very quickly. But little did they know they were in worse danger than ever before. The old woman was a wicked witch and she had decided to make Gretel work in the kitchen, and worst of all, she planned to fatten Hansel up so she might eat him!

The very next morning she locked poor Hansel in a big cage and gave Gretel a broom and told her to clean the gingerbread house from top to toe. In the evening, the witch fed Hansel a huge plate of chicken but she only gave poor Gretel a dry hunk of bread. But once she was asleep, Hansel shared his meal with Gretel. And so they lived for many days. The witch could not see very well. So every morning, the witch would make Hansel put his finger through the cage so she could tell how fat he was getting. But clever Hansel poked a chicken bone through the bars so she thought he was still too skinny to eat.

After many days, she grew fed up and decided to eat him anyway, and so she asked Gretel to help her prepare the big oven. The witch made some bread to go with her supper and when the oven was really hot she put it in to cook. The kitchen was soon filled with the lovely

smell of baking bread, and the witch asked Gretel to lift the bread out to cool. But Gretel was clever too. She pretended she couldn't reach the tray, and when the witch bent down inside the oven Gretel gave her a great shove and closed the door with a clang. And that was the end of the witch!

Gretel released Hansel, and together they set off once more to try to find their way home. After all their adventures, fortune finally smiled on them and they soon found the path home where they were reunited with their father who was simply overjoyed to see them again. And what, you might ask, of their mean mother? Well, the poor woodcutter had not had a happy moment since he left the children in the forest. He had become so miserable that she decided there was no living with him. The day before Hansel and Gretel returned, she had upped sticks and left, so that served her right, didn't it?

Snow White and the Seven Dwarfs

a retelling from the original tale by the Brothers Grimm

The queen was sitting at the window sewing, and thinking about her baby who would be born soon. As she sewed she pricked her finger, and red blood fell on the snow by the window ledge.

"I wish that my daughter be as white as snow, as black as ebony and as red as blood," she said to herself, and so it happened. Her tiny daughter had snow-white skin, lips as red as blood and hair as black as ebony, so she was called Snow White. But the queen died and the king married again. His new wife was very beautiful but she had a cold heart, and she did not love Snow White.

Every morning the new
queen would look into her
magic mirror and say,

"Mirror, mirror on the wall

Who is fairest in the land?"

and the mirror would always
reply,

"Thou, oh queen,

Thou art fairest in the land."

So the queen was content. Seven years passed and
Snow White grew into a lovely young girl, with her
mother's gentle nature.

One morning the queen looked into her mirror as
usual, but the mirror's reply filled her with a deep envy.

"Thou, oh queen,

Thou art indeed fair

But Snow White is the fairest in the land."

She ordered her woodsman to kill Snow White. But he could not bear to do such a wicked deed so he hid Snow White deep in the forest. Poor Snow White wandered about until she was utterly weary.

Suddenly, she caught sight of a light through the trees in the distance. It came from a little house with a lantern glowing in one small window. The door swung open at her touch, so she stepped inside. Everything was as neat as a new pin. A scrubbed wooden table was set, with seven plates and seven cups. Seven little chairs were ranged round the fireplace, and along the back wall there were seven little beds, each with a brightly coloured blanket.

There was a basket of logs beside the fireplace, and Snow White soon had a cheerful fire going. She sat in one of the little chairs and before long was fast asleep.

Now the cottage belonged to seven dwarfs and when they came home that evening, they were very worried to

discover Snow White fast asleep. They tiptoed round preparing their supper, but as the wonderful smell of stew filled the room, Snow White awoke with a start. She was very surprised to see seven little faces looking at her, but soon she was telling them how she came to be in the forest. They were very angry when they heard about the wicked queen.

"Might I stay with you?" asked Snow White. "I could look after you, and have supper ready for you every night."

The dwarfs were just delighted with this suggestion, and immediately set about making Snow White her own chair by the fireside and her own bed.

Back in the castle, the queen looked into her mirror in the morning, and asked,

"Mirror, mirror on the wall,

Who is fairest in the land?"

But you can imagine her rage when the mirror replied,

"Thou, oh queen,

Thou art indeed fair,

But Snow White with the seven dwarfs does dwell

And she is fairest in the land."

So the wicked queen disguised herself as an old pedlar, and searched out the dwarfs' cottage. Snow White did not recognise the queen and invited her in.

"Goodness me, you need new laces for your dress," said the old woman, and she pulled the new laces so tightly that Snow White was unable to breathe.

When the dwarfs came home that evening, they were horrified to discover Snow White lying on the floor as if

dead. They lifted her up and, of course, saw the laces. They quickly cut the tight cord and the colour came back to Snow White's cheeks.

"Now you know the queen will stop at nothing," they cried. "You must not let anyone indoors again."

The queen looked in her mirror the next morning, and went white with rage when it told her Snow White was still the fairest in the land. She disguised herself as a gypsy, selling wooden pegs and combs. Snow White remembered what the dwarfs had said and would not open the door. But the gypsy passed one of the combs through the window, and the minute it touched her hair, Snow White fell down in a faint for the comb was poisoned.

When the dwarfs came home and found Snow White, they immediately suspected the queen. They found the comb and pulled it out, and Snow White sat up, quite recovered. They pleaded with her to be more careful the next morning when they setoff for work.

So when a farmer's wife appeared trying to sell apples, Snow White would not even open the window.

"Why, anyone would think I was trying to poison you," said the farmer's wife, who was, of course, the wicked queen in disguise.

"I only want to give you some apples. Look how juicy they are!" and she took a big bite out of one.

So Snow White thought it must be all right and she took the apple. But the queen had poisoned it on one side only, and as Snow White took a bite she fell down dead.

This time when the dwarfs came home, there was nothing they could do. Snow White was indeed dead. They could not bear to bury her in the cold earth so they placed her in a glass coffin. They wrote her name on the side in silver and put the coffin in a sheltered part of the forest, and planted wild flowers all round about.

When the queen looked into her mirror the next morning, it gave her the answer she wanted.

"Thou, oh queen,

Thou art fairest in the land."

Years passed. Snow White lay in her coffin, looking as beautiful as ever. The dwarfs watched over her, and one day they found a young prince kneeling by the side of the glass coffin. He had fallen in love with Snow White the moment he had set eyes on her. When the dwarfs saw how deeply the prince felt about their beloved Snow White, they

agreed that he take the
glass coffin to his
palace where he
wished to set it
in his rose
gardens.

As the
prince lifted the
glass coffin, the piece of poisoned apple flew from her lips,
and Snow White opened her eyes. She saw the prince, she
saw her faithful dwarfs and she cried, "Where am I? What
has happened?"

There was huge excitement as everyone tried to talk
at once. The prince wasted no time and asked Snow White
to marry him. She agreed as long as the dwarfs could
come and live at the palace as well, and they all lived
happily ever after.

But what of the queen? She looked in her mirror the morning Snow White and the prince were to be married.

"Mirror, mirror on the wall

Who is fairest in the land?"

The mirror replied,

"Snow White, oh queen,

Snow White who marries her prince today,

She is fairest in the land."

The queen was so ugly in her rage that the mirror cracked from side to side. And she was never able to look in a mirror ever again as long as she lived.

Sleeping Beauty

a retelling from the original tale by Charles Perrault

Long, long ago, when fairies were still able to grant wishes, there lived a king and queen who wanted, more than anything in the whole world, to have a baby daughter. When their wish was finally granted and a beautiful tiny princess lay in her cradle, the king and queen decided to have a great candlelit party to celebrate. They invited the twelve most important fairies in the land and a great many other people besides.

As well as the thousands of glittering candles, there were golden tables piled high with all kinds of delicious food, and the royal orchestra played their most cheerful tunes. The twelve fairies all lined up to present their christening gifts to the tiny princess. Their gifts were those that only a fairy can give: beauty, kindness, grace, honesty and the like. The princess smiled happily in her cradle as one by one the fairies tiptoed up.

The eleventh fairy had just promised the princess a sweet singing voice, when there was a great roll of thunder and all the candles flickered out.

There stood quite the most wicked fairy anyone had ever seen. She was dressed all in black, her long straggly hair was black and her eyes, glittering in rage, were as black as the crow's feathers. Her voice was like a saw as she screeched, "How dare you not invite me to the party! I too have a gift for the little princess," and she smiled a not very nice smile. "Because you have forgotten me, my gift is that when the princess is sixteen she shall prick her finger on a spindle and die!" and with a horrid laugh, the wicked fairy disappeared with another clap of thunder.

As the candles were hastily relit, everyone started talking at once. Then a quiet voice was heard over all the hubbub. It was the twelfth fairy.

"I cannot undo this

wicked spell," she whispered, "but I can decree that the princess will not die. She will instead fall into a deep sleep for a hundred years," and all the fairies slipped away leaving the court in despair.

The king, of course, immediately ordered that all the spinning wheels in the land were to be burned. After a while, everyone grew less frightened, and as the princess grew up into the most lovely girl, the wicked fairy's prediction slipped from most people's memories.

On her sixteenth birthday the princess went exploring. At the top of a tower she did not remember seeing before, she found an old woman, sitting at a spinning wheel.

It was, of course, the wicked fairy in disguise. The princess was fascinated and, as she bent forward to look at the cloth, her hand caught the sharp spindle and she immediately fell to the ground as though dead. With a

swirl of smoke and a nasty laugh, the wicked fairy
disappeared.

Everyone else in the palace fell asleep at the same
moment. The king fell asleep with his ministers, the queen
and her maids fell asleep in her dressing room. The cook
fell asleep in the kitchen in the middle of baking a cake,
the groom fell asleep as he fed the horses in the stables and
even the little linnet the princess had in a golden cage by
her bedside fell asleep on its perch. A great high thorn
hedge grew up and soon the palace was completely
hidden. Time stood still and all was silent.

Many, many years passed. The tale of the sleeping
princess spread far and wide, and many came to try to find
her. But no one could get through the thorn hedge. And so
after even more years, people forgot what lay behind
the hedge.

Then one day a handsome prince came riding

through the woods, and as he reached the thorn hedge, thousands of pink roses burst into bloom. The prince walked forward, and a path appeared leading through the hedge towards the palace. It was a hundred years to the day since the princess had pricked her finger. The prince was astonished by the sight that met his eyes. Everywhere people lay asleep, frozen in the midst of whatever they had been doing when the spell caught them.

The prince climbed the tower, and there he found the princess, looking as lovely as ever. He bent over and kissed her, and immediately the spell was broken. The king and his ministers carried on just

where they had left off. The queen chose which dress she wanted to wear and the maids brushed her hair. The cook put her cake in the oven and the groom led the horses out into the courtyard. And even the little linnet in her golden cage sang a joyful song.

As for the princess . . . ! Well, she and the prince had fallen in love with each other on the spot, and were married the very next day. They all lived happily ever after, and the wicked fairy was never ever seen again.

Aladdin and the Lamp

a tale from The Arabian Nights

Aladdin's father had died years ago, abandoning Aladdin with no education, no job and no money. And so Aladdin lived life as a street urchin until there was a knock at his mother's door one evening and in strode a tall, turbaned man with a flowing cloak and the longest moustache Aladdin had ever seen.

"May Allah be praised! At last I have found you both!" the man cried, smiling broadly at Aladdin's mother. "I am Aladdin's long-lost uncle, a wealthy merchant, and I offer my nephew Aladdin the chance to come and work for me and make his fortune."

At this, Aladdin's mother's eyes opened wide and round. "I'm sure your father never mentioned a brother," she hissed under her breath to her son. "But don't be so foolish as to point it out!" And she set about making the merchant truly welcome.

Next morning, Aladdin was horrified to find that he was woken up at sunrise, forced to wash and tidy his hair, and pushed out of doors to begin his new career. Still half-asleep, he ran to keep up with his so-called uncle as he strode at a cracking pace through the bazaar, past the harbour, and right into the burning hot desert. "Find some wood and build a fire," his uncle ordered, and from the tone of his voice, Aladdin thought it was best not to argue. His uncle scattered some strange-smelling powders into the flames and chanted words in a weird language. There was a blaze of green fire and the ground trembled. When the smoke cleared, a trapdoor had appeared in the earth.

Aladdin's uncle heaved it open and bellowed at Aladdin, "Go down and find me a lamp!"

Aladdin was frozen with fear. His teeth chattered and his knees knocked with terror at all that had happened.

"You useless boy!" Aladdin's uncle roared, sounding highly like Aladdin's mother. He took a ring from his hand and shoved it roughly onto Aladdin's finger. "This magic ring will keep you safe. Now go!" And he pushed Aladdin through the trapdoor and onto the staircase.

Down, down, down into the darkness went Aladdin. He hurried through several gloomy caves and finally reached a beautiful garden. Many trees were growing there, covered in brightly coloured fruits. Aladdin couldn't resist picking handfuls of the glassy fruits and filling his pockets and shirt. He gasped with relief as he saw a rusty lamp resting on the grass, and he stuffed that into his shirt too. Then he was off back through the caves . . .

Now Aladdin hadn't spent all that time on the streets without becoming very streetwise. He was highly suspicious about his so-called uncle and, of course, Aladdin's suspicions were right. The merchant was in fact an evil sorcerer who knew powerful black magic. The sorcerer's wicked arts had shown him the whereabouts of the cave and the powers of the secret lamp that lay within, and he had worked hard for years to try to find a way in. Eventually, the sorcerer discovered that no one was allowed to enter the cave and take the lamp for themselves.

Someone else had to do it for them – someone like a street-urchin, who wouldn't be missed. Because that someone had to remain locked in the cave forever!

Now Aladdin could see the sorcerer's eyes glinting greedily down through the square hole that led to the upper world. "Give me the lamp!" the sorcerer barked.

All Aladdin wanted to do was to get out of there as quickly as possible. "Help me out first and then I'll give it to you," he shouted back.

"I said, give me the lamp!" the sorcerer insisted.

Aladdin wasn't stupid. "Sure," he yelled, "just as soon as you get me out of here!"

"GIVE ME THE LAMP, YOU STUPID BOY!" roared the sorcerer.

Well, that did it. Aladdin hated people telling him he was worthless. "NO!" he shouted. "I found it and now I'm going to keep it!"

The sorcerer hopped about with rage, cursing and spluttering. "Then have it," he screamed, "and enjoy it in the darkness forever!" He thundered out the magic words and the trapdoor slammed shut with a massive crash. When Aladdin put his hands up and felt about, the opening was gone.

"What have I done!" Aladdin moaned, wringing his hands. As he did so, he happened to rub the sorcerer's ring. There was a blinding flash and a huge genie stood before him.

"I am the genie of the ring!" the massive apparition thundered. "Speak your wish, O master, and I will obey."

"I wish to heaven I was out of this cave!" Aladdin howled.

At once, Aladdin found himself back on the sands of the desert, blinking in the hot sunlight. He raced home and blurted out his whole sorry adventure to his mother. At first she thought he was telling one of his usual stories, but then Aladdin showed her the multi-coloured glass fruits and rusty old lamp.

"If we sell these glittery baubles and this old lamp," his mother sighed, "we'll at least have some pennies to buy some bread and cheese to go with our soup tonight."

"But we won't get the best price for the lamp unless I try to clean it up a bit," said Aladdin. He picked it up and began to rub at it with his sleeve.

Once more, there was a blinding flash and a genie even bigger than the genie of the ring stood before him. "I am the genie of the lamp!" roared the enormous spirit. "Speak your wish, O master, and I will obey."

"Bring us some food!" was the Aladdin's command.

Suddenly there was a table before them, covered with huge golden platters laden with delicious food. Aladdin and his mother could hardly believe their eyes. In a few minutes, their stomachs were more full than they had been in years. And after they'd sold one of the gold platters in the market, their purses were too.

After that, the lives of Aladdin and his mother changed for the better. They were clever not to arouse suspicion by selling the gold platters only one at a time, when their purses were becoming empty. No one would have called them rich, although they lived much more comfortably than they had before. And so life would probably have gone on, if Aladdin hadn't been caught up in town one day in a great procession. Hundreds of slaves with swords at their sides came marching through the bazaar, and in the middle of them, high on their shoulders, was a magnificent litter of gold and silver. As the litter was carried past Aladdin, the swishing silk curtains swung just a little to one side, and inside Aladdin glimpsed the beautiful Princess Balroubadour.

From that moment on, Aladdin was head over heels in love. He couldn't speak, he couldn't eat, he couldn't sleep, for thinking of the beautiful Princess Balroubadour. Aladdin's mother watched her son grow thinner and paler by the day, and finally decided she had to do something about it – even if it was the most foolish thing she had ever done in her life. She loaded up one of the golden platters with the coloured, glassy fruits that Aladdin had brought back from the sorcerer's cave, and she went to see the princess's father – the Sultan of Baghdad himself!

Of course, the sultan realised what the jewels were at once – and he had never seen such huge, fine diamonds, emeralds, rubies and sapphires in his life. Being a greedy man, and hoping that there were more where those came from, he agreed at once that Aladdin should marry his daughter and become his son-in-law. Aladdin was overjoyed, and that night he dared to use the lamp once more and conjure up the genie. By morning, a splendid palace with golden domes and pearl spires and nine hundred and ninety-nine stained glass windows had been built exactly opposite the sultan's own palace. The sultan clapped his hands with delight, the wedding festivities were held that very afternoon, and Aladdin took his beautiful bride to live in his splendid new home.

It was fortunate that Princess Balroubadour felt the same way about Aladdin as he felt about her, and together they were completely happy – until one day, when Aladdin was out hunting, a ragged old pedlar came through the streets of the bazaar shouting, "New lamps for old! New lamps for old!" The princess and her maid rushed to the eighty-eighth window of the palace to look out on the funny little man who was offering to swap good wares for bad.

"How silly!" the maid giggled, and rushed to exchange the rusty old lamp in Aladdin's room. As soon as Aladdin's lamp was in the pedlar's hands, he gave a little cry of excitement and disappeared through the streets. A few seconds later, the princess, her maid and the entire palace had vanished, too! As you have probably guessed, the pedlar was none other than the wicked sorcerer.

Aladdin returned from his hunting trip to find his

wife missing, his palace gone and his father-in-law furious!
"Bring me my daughter within forty days," the Sultan
roared, "or I'll stuff your precious jewels into your mouth
and make you eat them!"

Worst of all, Aladdin no longer had his wonderful
lamp. "What am I going to do?" he moaned, standing all
alone in the spot where his palace had once been. He
wrung his hands in despair, and as he did so, he rubbed the
sorcerer's magic ring. In a flash, the genie of the ring stood
before him once more. "Speak your wish, O master, and I
will obey," boomed the mighty spirit.

"Bring back my palace, with everyone and
everything in it!" yelped the delighted Aladdin.

But the genie shook his head firmly and said, "I
cannot, master. The palace is under the power of the genie
of the lamp."

Aladdin thought hard for a couple of seconds and

then his face brightened. "Then take me to my wife!" he yelled.

Suddenly, Aladdin was standing in his palace in front of his startled – but overjoyed – wife. "Hurry," Princess Balroubadour urged. "The sorcerer is out at the moment, but he keeps the lamp with him at all times. We have to think of a way to get it from him."

The quickwitted Aladdin mixed a sleeping powder into a goblet of wine, gave it to the princess, and then hid behind a screen. Only a few moments later, the sorcerer came striding in, his cloak billowing out behind him. The smiling Princess

Balroubadour rushed to offer him a refreshing drink – and as soon as the sorcerer had thirstily drained the sleeping potion, he collapsed on the floor in a crumpled heap.

Aladdin sprang out from behind the screen and fumbled in the sorcerer's clothes. At last, he held his wonderful lamp in his hands! He rubbed it . . . gave the order . . . and in the twinkling of an eye, he, his wife, his palace – and the sorcerer – were back in Baghdad.

Aladdin and Princess Balroubadour breathed a sigh of relief. "I don't know about you," Aladdin said to his beautiful bride, "but I've had quite enough magic for one lifetime – and besides, now I've got you, I've got everything in the world I could possibly want." The princess nodded her agreement, and Aladdin once more rubbed his wonderful lamp. "I give you your freedom!" he told the genie, and in a blinding flash the overjoyed spirit was gone from the lamp forever.

Aladdin and the Princess Balroubadour (and of course, Aladdin's mum) lived happily ever after. And when the sorcerer eventually woke up, he got what he had always wanted – the rusty old lamp, no more and no less.

The Little Matchgirl

retold from the original tale by Hans Christian Andersen

I t was New Year's Eve and bitterly cold. Snow and ice lined the streets like an untrodden white carpet, for all the people were indoors, happily preparing to bring in the New Year. All alone in the windy square by the fountain, the poor girl who sold matches shivered. She pulled her ragged shawl a little closer around her thin cotton dress. She rubbed her hands together and blew on her fingers and stamped her feet, but freezing wet snow came swamping through the holes in her boots.

The little matchgirl hadn't sold one box of matches all day and she was too frightened to go home, for her father would be extremely angry. "Someone will surely pass this way and buy in a minute," she told herself. But how cold she was, how cold! "If only I could light one of my matches," she murmured, "that would warm me a little." With fingers stiff with cold, the little matchgirl falteringly took out one of her matches and struck it.

The tiny wooden splinter blazed into a bright little flame and the little matchgirl cupped her hands over it, craving its spark of warmth and light. As she stared into the orange centre of the flame, she saw herself standing in front of a roaring stove, giving out heat that warmed her from the tips of her toes to the top of her head. Suddenly, the match's flame went out and the vision died with it. The little matchgirl somehow felt even colder than before.

The little matchgirl didn't dare light another match for a long time. Then "Just one more," she whispered, through her chattering teeth. Shaking, the little matchgirl drew out another of her precious wares and struck it on the wall. The glimmer from the little matchstick seemed to light up the stone until it was clear and glassy, like a crystal window. Through the window, the little matchgirl could see a room with a welcoming fire and bright candles and a table laden with delicious things to eat, and she held out her hands towards it. It seemed as if she was going to be able to reach right through the glass and into the wonderful room – then the match died out. The magical room vanished, and huge tears filled the little matchgirl's eyes.

Her poor numb hands fumbled to light another, and her pale face lit up with wonder in the glow of the third flame. Suddenly a magnificent Christmas tree sparkled before the little matchgirl in the light. It shimmered with glassy balls of many colours and glittered with tinsel, and tiny dots of candlelight danced all over its thick green needles. "How beautiful!" breathed the little matchgirl, her eyes big and round. Then the match scorched her fingers and she dropped it, black and twisted, into the snow. The Christmas tree was gone, but the glimmering lights from its candles were still there, rising up and up into the night sky until they mingled with the twinkling stars. Suddenly, one of the lights fell through the darkness, leaving a blazing trail of silver behind it. "That means someone is dying," the little matchgirl murmured, remembering what her Granny used to say whenever they saw shooting stars.

As the little matchgirl stood dreaming of her beloved, dead grandmother, she unthinkingly lit up another match – and there was her granny before her in the light of the flame. "Granny, don't go!" sobbed the little matchgirl, as she lit one match after another, so the vision wouldn't fade like all the others. "Let me stay with you!" she begged, and the old lady smiled and held out her arms for the little matchgirl to run into, just as she always had done.

It was midnight, and all over the city the church bells pealed out to welcome in the New Year. Revellers poured out of the inns and houses to dance and sing and shake hands with strangers and wish each other well. There, lying in the snow by the fountain, was a little girl's thin, lifeless body, surrounded by spent matches. For the little matchgirl had left it there when she had gone away with her grandmother. She had no need of it in the place where they were going: a place without cold, nor hunger, nor pain – just happiness.

Thumbelina

retold from the original tale by Hans Christian Andersen

Once upon a time there was a woman who wanted more than anything in the world to have a child – but she didn't know where to get one. She went to see a witch about it and the witch gave her a special seed. The woman planted the seed in a flowerpot and it grew . . . and grew . . . and grew . . . into a bud that looked very much like the bud of a tulip. "What a beautiful flower!" the woman murmured one day, and she leant over and kissed the closed petals. POP! the bud exploded into an open flower, and there sitting in the middle of it was a tiny little girl, no bigger than the woman's thumb. The woman was overjoyed with her beautiful daughter and named her Thumbelina. The woman thought that her tiny daughter was utterly delightful and looked after her tenderly. But one night, a big, fat toad came hopping through a broken pane of glass in the woman's window. Hmmm, thought the toad, as her bulging eyes caught sight of Thumbelina sleeping in half a walnut shell. She would make a perfect wife for my son. The toad picked up the dreaming little girl, bed and all, and hopped away to the marshy river where she lived. The toad swam out to where the water ran fast and deep and placed Thumbelina in her walnut shell on a broad, flat lilypad. Now you can't run away, the toad thought, and she swam off to break the good news to her son . . .

When Thumbelina woke up and saw that she was not only lost, but trapped too, she began to cry bitterly. The fish wiggled up to see what was causing all the tiny splashes and ripples, and they took pity on the sad, tiny girl. Quickly and silently, they nibbled through the lilypad's green stem and Thumbelina went floating down the river.

Soon, she was far out of the toads' reach . . . and still the lilypad raft floated on. Thumbelina sailed past towns and was swept out into the countryside. Thumbelina liked it among the fields. It was sunny and peaceful, and a pretty white butterfly fluttered down to keep her company. Suddenly a large flying beetle dive-bombed the lilypad and wrapped his legs around Thumbelina's tiny waist. In a flash, Thumbelina found herself sitting on a twig with the beetle high up in a tree, watching her lilypad drift away without her.

Hundreds of the beetle's curious friends came crawling out of the bark to peer at what he had brought home. "Urgh! Look, it's only got two legs," the beetle children squealed.

"Where are its feelers?" some of the lady beetles murmured.

"Hasn't it got a slim bottom?" other lady beetles gasped in horror, admiring their own round shiny ones.

"It is rather ugly," the male beetles had to admit. "Let's get rid of it." And they flew down from the tree with Thumbelina and sat her on a daisy.

Poor Thumbelina felt very like crying. But just then she noticed a little hole in the earth below her that looked very like it was a type of doorway. She jumped down from the daisy and peered into the gloom. "Hello!" she cried. "Is anyone at home?"

After a few seconds, out popped a fieldmouse's head.

She looked Thumbelina up and down, and tutted loudly. "Dear, dear!" the fieldmouse scolded. "You look exhausted and hungry. If you're as lost as you look, you're very welcome to stay here with me – in return for keeping my rooms nice and clean and tidy."

So all winter Thumbelina lived with the fieldmouse. Every day, she washed and swept and scoured and polished, and the fieldmouse was very kind to her. Although, truth to tell, Thumbelina found life rather boring. The fieldmouse wasn't at all skilled at making entertaining conversation and neither was her regular visitor, Mr Mole. Mr Mole came once every week in his fine black velvet overcoat. He didn't like to talk. He just enjoyed sitting and peering at Thumbelina through his little, short-sighted eyes, and listening to her sing.

The fieldmouse was delighted that her friend so liked Thumbelina. "I think he's falling in love with you," she

whispered to
Thumbelina excitedly.
The fieldmouse was
even more sure that she
was right when Mr Mole
invited them both to visit
him in his splendid
underground mansion.

"I have dug a tunnel from your house to mine,"
Mr Mole informed them, "so you may come and see me
in comfort. Only please close your eyes when you are
halfway down the passage, for I am afraid that a dead
swallow is lying there."

Thumbelina wasn't at all revolted when she came
across the dead bird on her first trip to Mr Mole's house.
Instead, she felt pity for the poor thing, lying all stiff and
still on the cold earth. While the fieldmouse ran on eagerly

ahead, Thumbelina bent down and stroked the bird's feathers. "Goodbye, sweet swallow," she murmured, and she laid her head on the bird's soft breast. DUP! DUP! DUP! Thumbelina heard the swallow's heart beating – only very faintly, but Thumbelina knew that the bird was still just alive!

From then on, Thumbelina found as many excuses as possible to creep away from the fieldmouse and into the tunnel to care for the swallow. Over the weeks that followed, she placed leaves under the bird's head and plaited a coverlet of hay to keep it warm. She dripped drops of water into its weak throat and fed it tiny morsels of food – and gradually the swallow began to recover. By the time the weather had begun to grow warmer, the swallow was well enough to stand and hop about. On the first day of spring, the swallow was totally better – and extremely grateful for all Thumbelina's kindness. "One day,

I will repay you," he twittered as he hopped up the passageway and soared off into the blue sky.

It was then that the fieldmouse announced to Thumbelina that she had arranged for her to be married to Mr Mole. "He is very wealthy and will take good care of you," the fieldmouse beamed.

But Thumbelina was horrified. "I cannot live my life underground!" she cried, and ran sobbing out into the fields. She held her hands up to the sunshine and looked all around at the flowers, and she felt as if her heart would break.

Just then, Thumbelina heard a familiar twittering above her head. She looked up and saw her friend the swallow swooping down towards her. "Come away with me," cried the swallow, "I know a place where you will be happy. I have seen it on my travels." Joyfully, Thumbelina jumped onto his soft, feathery back.

The swallow flew off with Thumbelina over villages and roads, lakes and forests, snow-capped mountains, to a land where the weather was always sunny, where the breeze was always warm, and where in every flower there lived a tiny person just like Thumbelina. Thumbelina was very happy in her new home. She even married a handsome prince who lived in a rosebud and who was extremely glad that she had never become Mrs Mole! Best of all, the swallow came to visit every year in September, and stayed with Thumbelina and her prince each winter long.

Babushka

a Russian folk tale

There was great excitement in the village where Babushka lived. All the old lady's neighbours were out of doors, peering up at the wintry night sky, where the biggest star anyone had ever seen was shining down at them. "Where has it come from?" everyone gasped in astonishment. "What does it mean?"

Only Babushka stayed indoors, getting on with her housework as usual. "What a lot of fuss about a star!" she muttered as she swept and dusted, polished and tidied. "I haven't got time to waste, I've got standards to keep up." Babushka's house was always spotless and in perfect order.

RAT-TAT-TAT! came a loud knocking at the door.

"Now who's that interrupting my work?" Babushka frowned. She hurried to the door, plumping up the cushions and tidying a vase of flowers on the way. To her astonishment, three foreign-looking men were standing on the doormat, wrapped in long, embroidered robes and swathed in turbans. Even more surprisingly, the camels they had been riding were tied to the gatepost and were snorting puffs of steam into the crisp, cold air.

"Good evening, Babushka," the first man greeted her. He held out his hand and it jingled with bangles of gold, while jewelled rings sparkled on his fingers. "We are travelling from a far distant country, and we need a place to rest for the night. Would you be kind enough to welcome us in?"

Babushka could clearly see that the men were rich and important. "Of course . . . I would be honoured," she spluttered red-faced, and she welcomed her guests into her little sitting room while she quickly untied her apron and smoothed down her hair.

"What brings you to these parts?" Babushka asked politely, as she bustled about lighting a fire.

"We are following the strange star that shines so brilliantly," the second man explained.

"Really?" smiled Babushka, as she went to bring three plates of bread and cheese and pickles from the kitchen.

"We believe that it will lead us to a new king – the king of all heaven and earth," continued the third man.

"Well, fancy that!" remarked Babushka, scurrying to fetch three steaming mugs of hot chocolate.

"Why don't you come with us, Babushka?" the first man urged. "We will be leaving tomorrow with our gifts of gold, frankincense and myrrh."

"Thank you, but I can't possibly come with you," said Babushka. "If I were to go away, who would air the beds and sweep the stairs and dust the shelves and scour the sink? Besides, I don't have anything that would be suitable as a gift for a king!"

"This king is newborn," the second man said kindly. "He is still only a tiny baby."

Babushka paused with a tray full of washing-up. "I had a baby boy once," she said in a whisper, "but he died."

The third man rose to his feet and put his hand gently on Babushka's arm. "Come with us," he said, softly. "Come with us to see the baby saviour of the world."

Babushka stood and thought for a while. Her eyes had a faraway look in them and there was a sad smile on her lips. "Maybe just this once . . ." she murmured to herself. Suddenly – CUCKOO! CUCKOO! CUCKOO! – the clock in the hall noisily broke the silence. "Oh dear, is that the time?" cried Babushka, springing back into action. "I must go and make up the guest beds!" and she sprang off up the stairs.

Next evening, the star shone brighter and higher in the sky than ever. "Are you sure you won't come with us, Babushka?" the three men pleaded as they mounted their camels ready to go.

"I'd love to, but I've got too much to do," the old lady blustered.

The three men waved sadly as they lurched away. Babushka's heart was strangely heavy as she shut the door and went back inside her little cottage. She left her broom standing in the corner, the washing-up in the sink and the crumbs under the table, and she went and unlocked a cupboard in the corner of the sitting-room instead. Babushka sighed a deep sigh as she gazed at the shelves in front of her. They were stacked with toys of every size and colour. Babushka ran her fingers lovingly over them, wiping off a layer of dust. "My little son's toys would make a perfect present for the new baby king," she murmured.

It took Babushka all night to wash and dry and polish all the toys, until every single one was as good as new. As the sun came creeping through her window, she packed the toys in her shopping bag, put on her overcoat and headscarf, opened her cottage door and locked it behind her. Then she was off down the path.

Babushka walked and walked and walked – through villages and towns and cities. She lost all track of time, but she noticed one night that the star faded from the sky. A few days later, she came to the little town of Bethlehem. "Have you seen three men on camels, looking for a baby?" Babushka asked a local innkeeper.

"Why, yes," replied the innkeeper. "The three men were here all right. In fact, the baby was born in that very stable over there." He pointed to a dingy hut at the back of his inn. "The three men didn't stay long – just as well, really, because just after they'd gone, a group of shepherds came to see the baby too." The innkeeper laughed.

"It would have been a bit crowded with everyone there at once! But I'm afraid you're a bit too late. After the visitors had gone, the parents left with their baby last week."

Babushka looked from the empty stable to her full bag of toys. "I will go on searching until I find the baby," she decided. "I will give him my presents and ask him if he will be my king too." Then she turned on her heel and strode away determinedly . . .

Babushka is still wandering over the world today, looking for the baby king. No one notices her as she goes quietly from house to house, but whenever she sees a good girl or boy, she dips into her shopping bag and places a toy by their bed. It is only on one day every year that the children find Babushka's gifts — and that is Christmas Day, the birthday of Jesus, the baby in the stable.

Rip Van Winkle

an American legend

In a village in the foothills of the Catskill Mountains
of America lived a man called Rip Van Winkle.
Everybody liked Rip. He was a generous, easy-going
man who was always glad to lend a hand to his
neighbours. In fact, Rip Van Winkle was always to be
found doing anybody else's work except his own. And
didn't his wife remind him about it all the time! Nag, nag,
nag it was, all day long. "Rip, if you're not too busy
varnishing Mrs Green's fence today, you can mend the
holes in the shed. Instead of helping to burn the farmer's
rubbish, you can feed the chickens and milk the cows.

Then if you can stop yourself from building Arne Jacob's wall for him, there's our potatoes to dig up and the wagon to be washed down and the gutters to be cleared out and the yard to be swept and . . ." And so it was every day, on and on and on and on.

Every now and again, Rip Van Winkle whistled for his faithful dog Wolf, shouldered his gun, and strode away from his wife without a word. Off he would stroll up the mountainside, along the river and through the pine forests until his wife's screeching voice had grown so faint that he could no longer hear it, and he was surrounded only by the twittering of the birds, the rustling of the trees in the breeze and the panting of his companion by his side. Rip always knew there would be heck to pay when he got home. But a day off in the peaceful sunshine was well worth it!

One day when Rip had disappeared on one of these

rambles, he was taking a rest under a shady tree, when he heard a voice calling his name. "Rip Van Winkle! Rip Van Winkle! Rip Van Winkle!" came the high, shrill cry.

Wolf's ears flattened against his skull and he gave a long, low growl. Rip looked in the direction Wolf was snarling and there among the long grass was a nodding green feather. The nodding green feather was tucked into a bright red cap. The cap was on the head of a bearded man no higher than his own boot, struggling under the weight of a big beer barrel.

"Rip Van Winkle! Rip Van Winkle! Rip Van Winkle!" shouted the dwarf, crossly.

"Will you get yourself over here and give me a hand with this barrel before it squashes me!"

Rip was so used to doing what he was told that he jumped up to help at once.

"That's better," wheezed the dwarf, as Rip took one

end of the heavy barrel. "Now up we go!" Rip nearly tripped over as the dwarf stomped away up the mountain, pulling the barrel and Rip Van Winkle with him.

After at least an hour's tramping and much huffing and puffing, the dwarf led Rip Van Winkle straight behind a thundering waterfall, through a hidden door and into an enormous cavern.

Dwarfs were swarming everywhere. Some were dressed in aprons, pouring endless tankards of beer out of big kegs just like the one Rip was helping to carry.

Others were playing nine pins, rolling smooth round black rocks at copper skittles and cheering loudly. Yet more dwarfs were drinking and clinking their tankards together, singing noisy songs.

"Pull up a chair," Rip's new friend invited him, lowering the barrel to the floor and passing him a tankard. "Help yourself to a drink. You must be gasping thirsty after that climb – I know I am!"

The stunned Rip Van Winkle did just that. "My, that's mighty powerful stuff!" he spluttered, as he swallowed down a huge gulp of the dwarf beer. "But whatever it is, it's very good!" He licked his lips and poured himself another tankardful. None of the dwarfs was taking a blind bit of notice of him, so Rip Van Winkle sat back and began to watch the nine pins competition. "Well, this is a most pleasant way to spend the afternoon," he thought, helping himself to another beer . . . and another . . . and another . . .

and another. And before Rip Van Winkle even realised he was drunk, he had slumped forwards onto a huge flat rock and was snoring loudly.

When Rip woke up, the dwarfs were gone and the cavern was empty. "Come on, Wolf," he yawned, and they both stood up and stretched. "We'd better hurry back or we'll never hear the last of it." Through the little door they strode and out from behind the waterfall and off down the mountain. "Wait for it," he murmured to his dog as he climbed the porch steps to his house. "Any minute now, that wife of mine will start screeching fit to wake the dead." Rip put his hand on the doorknob and turned. He nearly walked smack-bang into the door as it failed to open. "Well, this needs a bit of oil," he murmured to himself. He rattled the knob and twisted it about. "Funny," Rip remarked, "I think it's locked. She never locks the door, never."

At that very moment, the front door opened and there stood a woman with an angry face. "Who are you?" the woman snapped. "What are you up to, trying to get in my front door?" She was not his wife. In fact, Rip Van Winkle had never seen her before.

"Who are you?" gasped Rip. "What are you doing in my house?"

"Your house!" the woman scoffed. "I've lived here for over nineteen years!"

Rip Van Winkle backed off the porch and looked around him. He scratched his head and stared. The woman was right – it wasn't his house. Well, it looked similar to his house, but the curtains at the window were different.

There were strange chairs
on the verandah. The
wagon in the yard
was not his wagon.

"But – I – How –"
stuttered Rip. "Where's Mrs Van Winkle?"

"Mrs Van Winkle?" the puzzled
woman gawped. "She left here nearly twenty
years ago, just after her husband wandered off
and disappeared. Now, be off with you or I'll
call the police!"

"Twenty years!" marvelled Rip Van
Winkle, as he wandered away stroking his
beard. His beard! Suddenly Rip realised that
his beard hung down to his knees. The woman's
words had to be true! He had been
asleep for twenty years!

Rip Van Winkle's hands trembled with the shock as he reached down and patted the bemused Wolf comfortingly. Then his mouth began to curve upwards in a small smile. "Just imagine, Wolf," he murmured. "No more nagging – ever!" Rip Van Winkle turned and strode across the street, whistling a merry tune. Happily, the inn was in the same place it always had been – and when the townspeople heard his story, he never had to buy himself another pint of beer again.

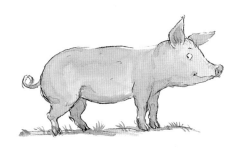

The Old Woman and Her Pig

a traditional folk tale

Long ago, an old woman found a bright, shining sixpence and went to market to buy a pig. She set off home with the pig trotting quite happily at her side. But when they were nearly there, they came to a stile and the pig wouldn't jump over it.

So the old woman went on a little further. She met a dog and said, "Dog! Dog! Bite pig. Pig won't jump over the stile, so I won't get home tonight." But the dog wouldn't.

So the old woman went on a little further. She met a stick and said, "Stick! Stick! Beat dog. Dog won't bite pig, and pig won't jump over the stile, so I won't get home tonight." But the stick wouldn't.

So the old woman went on a little further. She met a fire and said, "Fire! Fire! Burn stick. Stick won't beat dog, dog won't bite pig, and pig won't jump over the stile, so I won't get home tonight." But the fire wouldn't.

So the old woman went on a little further. She met some water and said, "Water! Water! Put out fire. Fire won't burn stick, stick won't beat dog, dog won't bite pig, and pig won't jump over the stile, so I won't get home tonight." But the water wouldn't.

So the old woman went on a little further. She met a horse and said, "Horse! Horse! Drink water. Water won't put out fire, fire won't burn stick, stick won't beat dog, dog won't bite pig, and pig won't jump over the stile, so I won't get home tonight." But the horse wouldn't.

So the old woman went on a little further. She met a

rope and said, "Rope! Rope! Lasso
horse. Horse won't drink water, water
won't put out fire, fire won't burn stick,
stick won't beat dog, dog won't bite pig,
and pig won't jump over the stile, so I
won't get home tonight." But the rope
wouldn't.

So the old woman went on
a little further.

She met a rat and said, "Rat! Rat! Gnaw rope. Rope
won't lasso horse, horse won't drink water, water won't put
out fire, fire won't burn stick, stick won't beat dog, dog
won't bite pig, and pig won't jump over the stile, so I won't
get home tonight." But the rat wouldn't.

So the old woman went on a little further. She met a
cat and said, "Cat! Cat! Scare rat. Rat won't gnaw rope,
rope won't lasso horse, horse won't drink water, water
won't put out fire, fire won't burn stick, stick won't beat
dog, dog won't bite pig, and pig won't jump over the stile,
so I won't get home tonight."

"All right," said the cat, " – if
you get me some milk."
The old woman was highly
surprised and fetched a
saucer of milk
at once.

The cat scared the rat, so the rat gnawed the rope, so the rope lassoed the horse, so the horse drank the water, so the water put out the fire, so the fire burnt the stick, so the stick beat the dog, so the dog bit the pig, so the pig jumped over the stile – and that's how the old woman got home that night!

The Brave Tin Soldier

retold from the original tale by Hans Christian Andersen

A little boy was once given a box of twenty-five tin soldiers as a gift. They wore smart uniforms and proudly shouldered their guns, and the little boy was very pleased with them. Only one of the tin soldiers wasn't quite perfect, for he had just one leg. He and his brothers had all been made from the same tin spoon, and there hadn't been quite enough metal to finish him off. Still, it was because he stood out as being special that the little boy put him to stand guard at the gates of the toy castle, instead of keeping him in the box with the others.

The tin soldier was very honoured to have been given an important duty, and he stood to attention, staring straight ahead. His gaze landed on a beautiful tiny doll whom the boy had placed in the open castle doorway. She was made of the very best plastic and wore a ballet dress of thin muslin, tied at the waist with a shiny blue ribbon. She held both her arms gracefully over her head and she balanced beautifully on one leg, for just like the tin soldier, she had one leg missing. (Well, in actual fact that wasn't the truth. The girl's other leg was extended out behind her because she was a dancer. But the tin soldier wasn't in a position to see it.) That would be just the wife for me, the tin soldier thought at least ten times every day. But the tin soldier dared not go and tell the girl of his love for her, for he was on duty.

One morning, the tin soldier was unexpectedly relieved of his post. A sudden breeze blew through the open window causing the curtains to flutter and knocking the soldier right off his feet and over the windowsill. Down he tumbled through the air, until he landed headfirst on the pavement.

The tin soldier didn't cry out for he was brave-hearted in the face of danger – not even when big drops of rain began to bombard him from above. So this is what it feels like to be out on the battlefield, the brave tin soldier thought.

Eventually the rain stopped falling and two keen-eyed boys came along and spotted the tin soldier among the puddles. The boys quickly folded some newspaper into a boat, popped the tin soldier in the middle, and set him afloat in the rainwater that rushed down the gutter at the side of the street. They ran alongside the boat as it swirled along, cheering it on its way delightedly. The tin soldier was shaking with fear inside, but he didn't flinch or move a muscle — even when the rushing water carried his newspaper boat down a drain and into the darkness under the pavement.

Suddenly a huge water-rat appeared. "Who goes there?" it demanded, twitching its whiskers and baring its long teeth.

At last, I face the enemy! thought the brave tin soldier. But before he could lower his gun and aim it, his newspaper boat was carried past the rat on the tide.

A glimmer of light appeared in the distance and the rushing of the water grew louder and louder. The tin soldier realised with horror that he was being swept towards a sudden drop where the drain water cascaded in a waterfall into a canal below. Even worse, the churning waters were splashing over the sides of the newspaper boat and the bottom was growing soggy beneath the tin soldier's feet. "Steady! Steady! Hold the line!" the brave tin soldier told himself. Suddenly the bottom of the boat ripped and gave way. The tin soldier plunged into the deeps and the icy waters closed over his head.

Surely now I am done for! thought the tin soldier, as he sank downwards through the murky wetness. Then all at once, everything went black as a fish swallowed him. The tin soldier choked and spluttered as he was gulped down into the fish's gullet, then the waters drained away and he was left lying on his back, holding tightly onto his gun. Even though the tin soldier couldn't see in the darkness, he could just about breathe in the stinking, rotten air. So this is what it's like to be a prisoner of war in a dungeon, the brave tin soldier thought to himself. To keep up his spirits, he concentrated on the beautiful dancing girl he had left at the castle.

The tin soldier lost track of time inside the fish, but eventually he was flung to and fro as the creature was caught on a hook and struggled to escape. Then everything went quiet and still for quite a while, until suddenly the fish was cut open. "I don't believe it!" came a voice "Here's the missing tin soldier," and a woman with a kind face reached in and pulled him out. She gave the brave tin soldier a shower under a running tap, carried him into the drawing room and set him back in his old position outside his very own castle.

The tin soldier puffed out his chest with pride. The war is over. I am back where I belong, he thought to himself. He stared straight ahead, and there was his love,

his sweetheart, the beautiful little dancing girl. Tomorrow,

as soon as I am off duty, I will definitely ask her to marry

me, the tin soldier decided. But then he felt an icy wind

around his ankles, and a breeze coming through the

window once more swept him off his feet and into the air.

This time he landed in the blazing flames of the open fire

– but the brave tin soldier didn't mind, for the dancing girl

was blown in too and landed at his side. "Be brave, my

love!" cried the tin soldier, holding his gun on his shoulder,

and the dancing girl burst into flames and was gone.

Then the tin soldier himself began to melt . . . and the

next day, when the woman with the kind face was raking

over the ashes, she found a tiny tin heart that the fire had

been unable to

burn away.

A Tall Story

an Indian folk tale

Five blind men were once sitting under a shady palm tree by the bank of the River Ganges in India, when they sensed that someone or something had silently crept up and joined them. "Who's there?" asked the first blind man. There was no reply, so he got to his feet and walked forwards with his arms outstretched. After a few steps, his hands hit something flat and rough and solid in front of him. "It's a wall!" he cried, triumphantly.

"Don't be stupid!" cried the second blind man,

standing up. "How could someone have built a wall right under our noses without us hearing?" He, too, felt about in front of him. "Aha!" he said, delightedly, as he ran his hands down a hard, smooth, stick-like thing. "It's a spear, definitely a spear!"

At that, the third blind man got up to join them. "A wall and a spear!" he sneered. "Obviously, neither of you have any idea what this thing is." His fingers closed around something tatty and wiggly. "It's nothing more than a piece of old rope!" he laughed.

"How can you say that?" argued the fourth blind man, who had jumped up and joined in without anyone noticing. "I'm standing here with my arms wrapped around something so big that my fingers are barely touching together.

It's a tree trunk, I'm telling you. A tree trunk!"

"I suppose I'll have to settle this," sniffed the fifth blind man, as he rose. He stuck out his hand confidently and grabbed hold of something long and swaying. "HELP!" he shouted. "It's a snake! It's a snake!"

Suddenly, whoops of laughter filled the air and the five blind men heard a little boy giggle, "You're ALL wrong! You're actually holding parts of an elephant – and you all look REALLY SILLY!"

At that, the first blind man stopped patting the elephant's side. The second blind man stopped stroking the elephant's tusk. The third blind man stopped holding the elephant's tail. The fourth blind man stopped hugging the elephant's leg. And the fifth blind man let go of the elephant's trunk. And from that moment on, the five blind men never argued again.